Advice to a Young Poet

Advice to a Young Poet

The Correspondence Between Llewelyn Powys

and Kenneth Hopkins

Edited by

R. L. Blackmore

Rutherford • Madison • Teaneck
Fairleigh Dickinson University Press

© 1969 by Associated University Presses, Inc.
Library of Congress Catalogue Card Number: 79-77089

Associated University Presses, Inc.
Cranbury, New Jersey 08512

8386–7348–1
Printed in the United States of America

To Lucia

Acknowledgments

For permission to quote from the following works, grateful acknowledgment is made to:
Malcolm Elwin for *The Life of Llewelyn Powys*, and, as literary executor, for the works of Llewelyn Powys.
Academic Center Library, The University of Texas, for unpublished manuscripts of Kenneth Hopkins.
Kenneth Hopkins, as literary executor, for the works of Louis Wilkinson.
Norma Millay Ellis for *The Letters of Edna St. Vincent Millay*, Harper and Row. Copyright 1952 by Norma Millay Ellis.
Laurence Pollinger Limited for the works of John Cowper Powys.
Colgate University Library for unpublished manuscripts of John Cowper Powys.
Francis Powys, literary executor, for Littleton Powys' *The Joy of It*, Chapman and Hall Ltd.

Contents

Illustrations

Introduction

My debts of gratitude are few, and very deep. During the editing of the letters, several people gave time and counsel that no verbal acknowledgment could properly acquit; their aid amounts to participation, so much so that these opening paragraphs are less a prefatory listing of names than an introductory posting of information central to an understanding of the correspondence between Llewelyn Powys and Kenneth Hopkins.

Alyse Gregory, who lived near Tiverton, in Devonshire, gave permission for this publication of her late husband's letters to Hopkins, and then, as questions of fact and interpretation arose, became my weekly correspondent. Few are the pages that do not reflect, in some way, her most graciously given advice. With English skill and New England patience she answered myriad questions about English ways and wordings, as I sought the connotations of phrases not common in America: Connecticut-born, she lived in New York City until her husband's ill health forced her to relinquish the managing editorship of *The Dial*, early in 1925, and return with him to his native Dorset. (The Powyses, too, needed help with colloquialisms beyond their ken: Theodore Francis, third eldest of the brothers, never quite grasped the new word for sports trousers, and referred to men playing golf in "all fours"; and in 1939 Llewelyn had to learn from his wife that the "phoney War" did not mean the mechanical way the world's leaders were communicating.) Despite Miss Gregory's anxiety to remain always in the background on matters not involving her own writings, she followed her husband's example in permitting publication of anything that seemed pertinent. In the 1949 edition of *Advice to a Young Poet*, which contained only Llewelyn Powys' share of the correspondence, certain omissions were then advisable. Now—with the single exception of the surname of an editor unjustly slurred after a book went astray in the mail—all deletions have been restored, and the letters that she herself wrote to Hopkins when her husband was too ill to write have been inserted in their proper places.

The sudden death of Alyse Gregory in August, 1967, at the start of her eighty-fourth year, takes a noble and sensitive spirit from the earth. Her cottage at Morebath still contains, as this book goes into production, a library whose inscribed books speak eloquently of the counsel and criticism she gave for so long to so many writers—books that range from a bound volume of *The Dial* of 1922 with the first issue of Eliot's "The Waste Land" to the most recent of monographs on Proust, whom she held highest among novelists. In her own home—in the books dedicated to her and inscribed to her by grateful authors— she had had the chance to know that gratitude directly. Few editor-writers have so fully earned such tributes.

My indebtedness to Kenneth Hopkins is great, in- deed. Perhaps an actual anecdote will best illustrate the value of having one's research at hand—in person. Several of the Hopkins papers at the University of Texas and two manuscript poems from 1938 in my possession carry marginal notations of Joyce's critical reactions to Hop- kins' poetry. I knew that Hopkins had not been, that year, on the continent; but he had been, always, a fecund ltter writer. Down came Richard Ellmann's books and Stuart Gilbert's edition of Joyce's *Letters*, but the Hop- kins indexed was Gerard Manley; the Powys, John Cow- per; the Gregory, Lady Augusta. The trail was the more exciting because Joyce proved, for me, a critic of acumen; I wholly agreed with the terse dismissal of a lusty little quatrain: "Joyce says no!" And on a delightful sonnet, "Speak to me now the kiss is done," the penciled words, in Hopkins' hand, were "Joyce liked this."

Then, mercifully sparing me protracted correspondence and perhaps even trips to the Lockwood Memorial Library at Buffalo and to the Houghton, Beinecke, and Cornell collections, Kenneth Hopkins arrived from England. "Joyce? Oh, yes. Joyce Honeywill read most of my things that year. A charming girl, but not much of a critic."

Few editors, I suspect, have had subjects so accessible, so helpful, and so generous with friendship as Kenneth Hopkins—and had, as lagniappe, a Hampshire guide (and Texas admiral) show them the south-central United States through a Greyhound bus window. Like Miss Gregory, he imposed no restrictions, wielded no blue pencil, demanded no emendations. Orthography was not a conspicuous virtue of Hopkins' early work. A kinder editor— or a petty author with the old MSS in his hands—might have quietly corrected "lovliness" and punctuated away the verbal ambiguity of the sonnet enclosed in his first letter to Llewelyn Powys, but he has permitted me to preserve these youthful *lapsi calami* exactly as he wrote them. Part of the vitality of the correspondence springs from contrast—contrasts in schooling, background, ways of life—and from the tutorial, and tutelary, tone of Powys' letters. "I feel inclined to give you some advice," he wrote after their first meeting, "as though you were my bastard and I Lord Chesterfield." The words of both men—the fifty-year-old Cantabrigian's and the twenty-year-old ironmonger's—stand as they wrote them, for I have allowed Powys' hasty and sometimes illogical habit of stringing sentences together with dashes to go unaltered. In an edition of letters readability is of course the cardinal grace, but it must not require the total sacrifice of tonal accuracy. Powys' rapid pen strokes and Hopkins' spellings may disturb some, but I think they will speak to many others.

And it is for readability that, wherever feasible, I have given up superior numbers and raised the stuff of many footnotes to linking blocks between the Powys-Hopkins letters. The correspondence has more value, I believe, for those interested in poets and writing than for professional scholars. It is, in fact, a narrative, one almost classically unified: The time is the years between this century's two world-wide wars, the twenty-one years that legally bring a body to maturity; more narrowly, the time is the economically depressed period, 1935 to 1939, that brought to a close, prematurely, the first half of the twentieth century. The characters are two, the novice and the sage. The place is the Republic of Letters, reaching from Dorset and London to the Alpine valley at Davos Platz, where, in modern times, so many consumptives, from Robert Louis Stevenson to Hans Castorp, have gone for recruital. And the theme is always writing, the craft of writing and an author's way of life.

It is by further happy chance that the oldest of the three surviving Powys brothers and sisters lives near Sneeden's Landing, New York. Marian Powys Grey, closest in age to Llewelyn, and retired now from her New York City business and her position as Consultant of Lace for the Metropolitan Museum, has given much of the flavor of their Somerset childhood for the chapter on the Powys family, but more important than any facts has been to hear her, in the garden of her home above the palisades of the Hudson River, read so impressively her brothers' words—even as her mother must have read to the family as they were growing up. Beyond any relevance to this book, I am grateful for the privilege of knowing a woman in her eighties who so abundantly confirms, as she lives alone with her books, her flowers, and her collection of lace, her profound and Powysian belief that the mature years can be fruitful and serene.

The Colgate University Library and the Humanities Research Center of the University of Texas are the depositories of manuscripts and letters basic to this book. To Bruce Brown, Thomas Davies, and the staff in charge of the Colgate Powys Collection, and to Warren Roberts and the custodians of the Texas Hopkins Collection I extend thanks. Today—when service has become a calculable commodity, a wedge in economists' pie-charts of the Gross National Product—libraries seem the sole surviving bastion where aid and counsel, purveyed with good coffee, are taken for granted as humane values.

Throughout this undertaking I have enjoyed the consistent encouragement and advocacy of Joseph Slater; indeed, the suggestion that the full correspondence be published was his. Through nearly three decades the staunch judgment and discerning taste of Earl Daniels have been constant check points. My appreciation for all he has done is deep-felt. And for help with specific questions I acknowledge the assistance, graciously given to a stranger, by Sylvia Townsend Warner and Walter Jackson Bate. To several others I am grateful for acts not directly related to the contents of this book: it was Norman H. Strouse, a lover of literature as well as of books, whose gift of Powys MSS to Colgate University planted the first seed of these pages; a grant from the Colgate Research Council financed more than half of my research expense; and the cooperation of Herman Brautigam, the late James Storing, and Vincent Barnett in rearranging my teaching schedule afforded consecutive hours, rather than stolen minutes, for this task.

Gentleman and scholar are common hackneyed now—words used as often as their prerequisites are rare—but the capstone of my good fortune during his tenure at Syracuse University was in having a mentor who is, pre-eminently, a scholar and a gentleman. With wholehearted admiration I express my gratitude to Cecil Y. Lang.

My dependence on Llewelyn Powys' biographers, Malcolm Elwin and the late Louis U. Wilkinson, shows on many pages. Wilkinson's *Welsh Ambassadors* (London, 1936) —written, like most of his books, over the name "Louis Marlow"—and his editing of *The Letters of Llewelyn Powys* (London, 1943) stand in full confirmation of Powys' words from Africa, in 1916, describing him as "still after everything dearest and noblest of my friends." Although Malcolm Elwin never met his subject, his *Life of Llewelyn Powys* (London, 1946) gives all the consecutive particulars, and is a warm appreciation—not an easy blending. These books—together with Hopkins' and Powys' works—are my primary published sources; for the last two I use the short titles, *Letters* and *Life*.

Advice to a Young Poet

1
The Urge to Write

An ailing English author in his fifties wrote forty-eight letters of advice, over a period of three and a half years, to an aspiring poet in his early twenties. One sentence—cut almost to the binary language of computing machines—summarizes the *facts* about the correspondence between Llewelyn Powys and Kenneth Hopkins, but a subjectivity that machines cannot cope with, yet, creeps in with the adjectives.

Kenneth Hopkins' compulsion to transcribe the teemings of his mind and heart shows in all his letters. There is rarely a paragraph—whether it means to reckon a girl's beauty or report a man's thirst for good beer—that does not loop back to the subject of writing. The analogies are not too strong: he was fevered to write, driven to publish, and it was this young apprentice of Hampshire who initiated the correspondence by asking to visit the sick writer in Dorsetshire.

Llewelyn Powys' urge to speak out also came early. After Cambridge (Corpus Christi) he tried the classroom and the American lecture circuit, and disliked the mechanics of both. Then, in his twenty-fifth year, he became tuberculous, and all he had to say thereafter was written; by the time of Hopkins' first letter he had published twenty-two volumes of essays, autobiography, philosophy, and fiction. Hemorrhages of the lungs recurred throughout his life, and when Hopkins' brash self-invitation arrived, Powys had been in bed for more than two years. His compliance suggests that he recognized at least the ardor of a twenty-year-old who would write, even in jest, of having "a higher opinion of my own value as a poet than any man in England."

But the very name Powys might vex a computer, for he and his ideas have always flapped formalists—in ethics, esthetics, religion. So successful was he in provoking those who were "shored and trussed and buttressed" in the Establishment that a major London daily—ignoring obituary courtesy in December, 1939—labeled him a "crank," his ideas "dangerous." After reading the death notices from all the world, his widow wrote:". . . the rank-and-file of accredited periodicals described him as a sick man, who, too sensitive to withstand the shocks of this disastrous world, had turned his own suffering into a system—fragile and shot through with pessimism—of breathless revolt."

The "dangerous" pessimist held these ideas:

Love life. Savor it fully. "Live! live! live!" command several letters to Hopkins. "To be happy is the true aim and the end of life." "Happiness can be won against all odds if we possess wisdom and imagination and a passionate unregenerate allegiance to the leap of life," he wrote in *Impassioned Clay.*

The first recourse was to the senses, with intelligence, not Providence, their guide. Spread before man is all this world—the bright and the dark, sunlight and storm cloud. Earth's bounty is for man's enjoyment. "The grain grows golden in its husk," he said of August, his birth month, in *Skin for Skin.* "The green apples swell on their whorled twigs, and the shell of each hazelnut is neatly fitted with its ivory kernel. What have we to fear?"

"Too many men and women spend their time between an office and a home in a state of intellectual stupor," he wrote in *Earth Memories.* "No human being should ever wake without looking at the sun with grateful recognition of the liberty of another day."

Nature is neither cruel nor kind, but insensible, incognizant. No man can hold otherwise, Powys said again and again, who has lived five years near Lake Elmenteita in British East Africa and heard the death screams of a lamb and then found the blood-drenched lion sleeping clean-conscienced. "Real wickedness is the substitution of dead values for living values." "Insensitivity is the cardinal sin." Willingly "to cause suffering, physical or mental, is the only unpardonable sin," he wrote in *Glory of Life*.

And love is supreme. "The emotions connected with love are by far the most profound that we ever experience," he wrote in the Introduction to *The Book of Days*. "It should be a matter of honour with hedonists to give encouragement and protection to lovers."

The "pessimist's" final written words went to another young English writer he was encouraging; the war-time postcard, sent eleven days before his death, says only this:

I shall be delighted, my dear John Rowland, to be associated with anything you write, whether of roguery, poetry, or philosophy. I believe with you that the present desolations will pass and you and your children will live in a better age with simplicity and gaiety. Dust is soft, secret, and silent. I am not so well, but have had a happy life for half a century in sunshine.

—Bless you
Llewelyn Powys

The danger that the London obituary writer found in Powys undoubtedly lay in his Epicureanism and its corollary disbelief in a future life: "Dead, dead, dead, all dead utterly forgotten. The treat is for the living." "The wise man recognizes a sacred obligation to each fleet moment." The canon is clear throughout all his books, and his saints are frequently invoked: Lucretius, Montaigne, the Preacher of Ecclesiastes, Homer, Shakespeare, Akhenaton, and Epicurus. "To rejoice in life, to find the world delightful to live in, was a mark of the Greek spirit which distinguished it from all that had gone before," Edith Hamilton wrote in *The Greek Way*. "To be versed in the ways of nature means that a man has observed outside facts and reasoned about them. He has used his powers not to escape from the world but to think himself more deeply into it." Llewelyn Powys' Hellenistic cast of spirit lay even on his visage as, during illness, he wore the beard shown in the photograph reproduced in this book. But he was "Epicurus owene sone" in the first sense, before Chaucer and before time turned Epicureanism full face from its ideal and tranquil prudence. Powys was more likely to fare sumptuously on Epicurus' Cythnian cheese than the Franklin's sauces, poignant and sharp.

The Cradle of God gives four injunctions: "Be generous, be free, be impassioned, be *understanding*." And there is some choice:

> Despite all that can be said by the fatalists, however, we have a kind of inch-long freedom of action, and limited though this freedom may be, it is sufficient. "It is not as wide as a church door," but it will sway to the stretch of a hedgehog's tail, and serves our turn well enough.
> *The Book of Days*

"The more we overcome our congenital apathy, our lumpish disposition to take for granted the deep mystery of existence," Llewelyn Powys wrote in *Damnable Opinions*, "the more do we fulfil the design of being alive." Life and the sun—in the form of the Egyptian hieroglyph that stands for both—appears on the covers of all but Powys' earliest books. And he had this ankh, Kenneth Hopkins tells, cast in six basic metals as gifts for his friends; Hopkins carried his sign of the sun for many years until the metal wore all away. This personal colophon, one of the most ancient of symbols, honors the giver, warmer, maintainer, ripener, and the guarantor of ephemeral life.

But Llewelyn Powys was more than an observer and

an absorber, counseling a full life under the sun. Although he never accommodated his "dangerous" views to others, he did not turn bigot or vindictively intolerant of those who saw the world differently. In all his letters to his oldest brother, John Cowper, who believed until his final years that there was a fifty-fifty chance of immortality,[1] no word is impatient as they debated the ultimate. But Llewelyn preached his doctrine with perhaps more fervor than his father, the Vicar of Montacute, preached his traditional, more widely held tenets. The very titles of the books named above are rallying cries for rationality, and the two nouns of *Love and Death*, an "imaginary autobiography" published just before Llewelyn's death, summarize what he found to be the best *in* life and the fruit *of* it. Important, too, was Llewelyn Powys' willingness to act on his beliefs. To chide dullness and insensitivity, to laud the bounty of nature, to celebrate the sun and the life it gives—these are verbal tasks. But far beyond mere talk is the story (told in a later chapter) of the fight he undertook against cruelty when he found it in his own shire.

That the adviser of *Advice to a Young Poet* was not himself a writer of verse may be paradoxical, but the briefest sampling of any of Powys' works reveals that his mode was always poetic—a rich mode that needs no shaping on the page to signal itself. Even in the letters he wrote so rapidly, no two dozen words go together without the hallmark of a true "maker." Nor was his counsel prosodic. There is no word to Hopkins about the forms of verse, no talk of meter or rhyme, of iambs or stanzaic form. There is almost no concern with content; Powys often "likes well" Hopkins' subject, but rarely says more,

---

[1] For John Cowper Powys' generally overlooked shift toward Llewelyn's view, see his introduction to the new edition of *Wolf Solent* (London, 1961; Hamilton, New York, 1966).

and only in Letters 43 and 45 does he raise an enthusiastic voice, when Hopkins writes a long Faustian poem that approaches Powys' own ideas. And, though any young poet might long for advice on how to market his verse, there is but one postscript giving a magazine address; balancing this are warnings against premature publication and the admonition, preliminary to writing a preface to Hopkins' poems, that "you must not expect me to say more than I feel." Most of the specific references, few as they are, are to diction.

Forgoing, then, matters of form and content and the stuff of literary textbooks and criticism, Llewelyn Powys counseled on matters of prime moment: on a poet's heart and senses and taste and judgment; on his ways of perceiving and apperceiving; on his development of empathy and cognitive insight; on the intensifying of his spiritual being:

> . . . try writing from your actual experience, converting into poetry the very dust of every-day life as poets can do, turning all into gold.
> . . . read, learn, meditate, live.
> . . . learn to *discriminate*.
> . . . leap like a grasshopper clean out of your skin and with an imaginative effort put yourself in [your reader's] place.
> . . . be much alone.
> . . . try to detach your own sensations, pure and naked, like leaping live fish, from the welter of traditional sensations and to express them.
> . . . do not talk nonsense about "inspiration."
> . . . have eyes for all.
> . . . never be content with the second rate.
> . . . [send] your soul from your wrist like a Merlin hawk to fly to the stars.
> . . . observe how the world wags in bawdy houses.
> . . . take notes, observe—write always.

The letters consider a poet's reins and his soul, not his tropes and syllables. The true subject of the correspondence is the highest possible concern for Llewelyn Powys: the poetic way of life.

While editing this correspondence, I asked two questions of several friends of Llewelyn Powys and Kenneth Hopkins: how did so ill a man, husbanding the strength of his last years for his own writing (seven books between 1935 and 1939), find the energy and the impulse to compose these lengthy letters, written mostly in bed on a pad held on his knee? And why to Hopkins, with whom he spent a total of less than five hours? My *whys* were disturbing, perhaps, to those who live in an older culture and find some truths—friendship among them—self-evident, and who distrust or scorn motive-probing by psychologists, or philologists. And it was patently true that Hopkins' charm, intelligence, and dedication to writing were sufficient reasons for so generous a response as Powys'. Alyse Gregory put it best in a letter:

> To answer your question about how my husband, when so *very* ill, consented to see Mr. Hopkins—he was always interested in and sympathetic to young people and I do not remember his ever refusing to see any stranger who had written in advance. . . . [Miss Gregory tells of several others who sought and received advice.] I think Mr. Hopkins was exceptional in that he had the ardour, pertinacity, and modesty to profit by all that my husband would teach him, and to persevere against great handicaps in the writing profession. I am sure my husband would be both touched and gratified were he alive today to know that his words had borne fruits, and to such an extent.

Beyond what Miss Gregory has said—but not conflicting with it, and in no way detracting from Llewelyn Powys' generosity or Kenneth Hopkins' poetic promise—there may be an answer that accounts for the tone and some of the phrases of Powys' letters, an answer suggested by several words quoted above: *canon, saint, celebrate,* and *in-*

voke. To wrench excerpts from a three-and-a-half-year correspondence is to give them deceptive emphasis, but phrases like these appear regularly: "regulate your life as strict as a religious devotee," "appreciation of the mystery," "separates you from the uninitiated," "in becoming a poet you enter the society of the most select company possible," "I will initiate you into these subtle secrets," "part of a religious rite."

But even this needs broadening. Life was the be-all and end-all for Llewelyn Powys, and the celebration of life was poetry. There were high-poets, but poetry reached far beyond its best makers—was something more awesome.

> With each of us it is the simple poetry of our hours, with their joys and their sorrows, that will count at last.
> *Damnable Opinions*
> The religion of poetry rests today, as it did in the time of Homer, on the impassioned appreciation of appearances.
> *Earth Memories*
> Steadfastly hold to the native poetry of life. It will be strong to sustain when all else fails.
> *Impassioned Clay*
> Some of us today are content to find the secret of life in poetry. Wonder remains still the homage that our nature pays to the unknown.
> *The Pathetic Fallacy*
> The secret of life lies in our own individual poetic vision.
> *Now That the Gods Are Dead*
> There are no miracles because *all is a miracle.* There is no magic because *all is magic.*
> *A Pagan's Pilgrimage*
> In the last analysis religion can be defined as a heightened awareness of the poetry of existence.
> *Earth Memories*

And so at Hopkins' instigation they met, these two who had little in common except the desire to write. In the following pages the manifestations and perhaps some few causes of the urge to write—Juvenal's "cacoëthes scribendi"

—will appear as I give the background of Kenneth Hopkins, and, more fully, of Llewelyn Powys and the prolific and controversial family of writers of which he was so much a part. I would begin by recasting the first sentence of this chapter, pushing it farther from the "binary" reach of computing machines: Before his death, a latter-day Epicurean, still joying in all life about him, instructed an aspirant in what he had found to be the highest order of this brief and single life: the calling of poet.

2

The Young Poet

One man wants to write, as another wants to climb mountains. Both are asked *why* in the same tone, perplexed and faintly querulous, and though writers still mumble or shrug, climbers have gone a leg up with Maurice Herzog's unexceptionable answer, "Because it's there." For Annapurna, as Shelley said of Mont Blanc, yet gleams on high: the power is *there*, visibly, demonstrably, unlike the pulses of a man's mind, the songs of his thinking heart.

Kenneth Hopkins' autobiography, *The Corruption of a Poet*, has a phrase that might almost stand with Herzog's declaration: "I Commence Author." It is the title of an early chapter that opens boldly:

> I wrote my first poem at seven or eight and won the applause of Auntie Sally. Only the last two lines have survived . . .
>
> And there in the beer cellar, where he had died,
> Lay the Butler, his throat slit, with fixed, horrid leer.
>
> Auntie Sally, who had been in service all her life, thought very highly of this and said she had once known a Butler in similar circumstances.

But the hard fact is that after this brave opening, and the quotation of one line from his first-published poem (he was ten when it appeared in the *Parish Magazine* of St. Peter's Church, Bournemouth), Hopkins shifts on the next page to the more tractable subject of Sunday-school picnics; for the autobiography is—he says in explaining, in the fourteenth chapter, the omission of his significant meetings and correspondence with Powys—but a "light-

hearted and superficial record of my days and to say what
these men [Llewelyn and John Cowper Powys] have
meant to me would be to introduce a wholly different
note."

Despite the withholding of some serious matter—for, I
assume, a later telling—*The Corruption of a Poet* pro-
vides much information about the early days. The title is
Dryden's, from the dedication to *Examen Poeticum*, and
its enrollment as Hopkins' epigraph and title is tersely
told in the jottings on an early Hopkins manuscript. In
the papers that he lent me—in the same packet with the
"Joyce" criticisms of his work—is a sonnet from 1937,
"Must you set forth our love for all to see"; in the margin is proof that Hopkins can never join the long list
of authors who claim never to read their own works once
they are finished. The sonnet carries a sequence of penciled, dated comments—four in all—in Hopkins' hand:

"bloody good—1940"
"bloody good—1941"
"bloody good—1942"
"*fairly* good, '46 (Cf. The corruption of a poet is the generation of a critic—Dryden) ."[1]

The sonnet, unchanged since 1937, is on page 90 of Hopkins' *Collected Poems: 1935–1965.*

Both Llewelyn Powys and Kenneth Hopkins were
"dipt in ink," but—aside from their choice of southern
England as a place of birth—they shared no common circumstances.

A Hampshireman, Hopkins was born in Bournemouth
on December 7, 1914, five months after his father had left
home for military service; he was five and in school before

---

[1] Twenty-five years earlier, in "A Defence of *An Essay of Dramatic
Poesy*" (1668) , Dryden had written, "The corruption of a poet is
the generation of a statesman."

his father returned from India and reopened a shoe-repair shop, four doors and some hundred feet down the street from where they lived. Later, his parents opened a small grocery store in the front room of their home, run by his mother, for the most part, after his father became the cobbler and playground supervisor of a Christchurch orphanage. Kenneth, the younger of the two children of this marriage (his sister was two years his senior, and an older stepbrother lived with them for a while), delivered groceries in a four-wheeled soap-box before graduating to a bicycle with a basket. A second job paid cash: choir-boy at St. Peter's, singing at ten services and four practices each week, not counting weddings and funerals.

Thirty miles to the west and thirty years earlier, Llewelyn Powys, the eighth of eleven children, was born at Rothesay House, "an enormously large dwelling in an extensive garden" rented from "a mayor of Hardy's *Casterbridge.*" In 1886, before Llewelyn was two years old, his father, the Reverend Charles Francis Powys (who had inherited some forty thousand pounds on the death of his older brother six years earlier), moved with his family to a large Victorian vicarage where he remained as Vicar of Montacute for a third of a century, until the end of World War I. Llewelyn's childhood, he said in *Somerset Essays*, written the year after he met Hopkins, seemed to have been lived partly in an eighteenth- and partly in a twentieth-century context, and he pointed out his father's rôle of working with two social classes:

> It has been for three generations the business of my family as country clergymen to stand between the landed gentry and the people of the village. . . . The Squire [of Montacute] was a highly cultured gentleman with a kindly disposition, but the traditions of his class were firmly fixed in him. He never questioned his right to be an autocratic ruler over the lives of all those who lived upon his hereditary acres, and the democratic assertiveness that became common

among the working classes toward the latter end of the nineteenth century was constantly resented by him.

Adjacent to the Vicarage—which remained Llewelyn Powys' fixed base during his various activities until he left for Africa at age thirty—was Montacute House. It "stirred my imagination," he wrote,

> the armory for example, with helmets and cuirasses used at the time of the Great Rebellion. . . . But most wonderful of all it was to step suddenly into the immense gallery that stretched one hundred and eighty feet from end to end of the house. . . . How swiftly on a rainy afternoon the time would go by in so spacious a playing room! The great rocking-horse was kept there, the highest-stepping dapple grey ever built by a carpenter. . . .

> The rain would beat against one or other of the high oriel windows at each end of the gallery, where, to the south, the village was overlooked, or where, at the other end, the stately ornamental North Gardens could be seen, with their dark drenched yew trees standing like royal sentinels against the meadows that rose into view beyond the privileged enclosure.

Adjoining all of Kenneth Hopkins' homes—until he left for London at age twenty-three—was Southern Railway property.

> Our part of Southcote Road contained bigger houses than the station end, and none of those commercial yards backing on to the railway behind the houses. In fact we backed on to the tram depot, and the railway lay beyond that. So we felt (anyway, I did) that ours was a very select area. . . .

> I had better sort out these several residences. I was born at 133. We lived during the war mainly at 41. We sometimes spent a night or so at 49 [Aunt Ada's] . . . and after my father came home from the war we bought 125, and that is still [1954, when *The Corruption of a Poet* was written] my mother's headquarters. So the family history for forty years has been enacted in this same Southcote Road—and always

on the north side which means houses facing south and getting the sun, but that much nearer to the railway with its
varied noises. . . .

The house [at 133] is one storey high, about sixteen feet
wide at the front, and tapers off to a point at the back. . . .
[125] had one attractive feature not found in the otherwise
identical 123, 127, and 129. It had a eucalyptus tree in the
front.

At fourteen, after finishing elementary school at St. Peter's,
Kenneth Hopkins was apprenticed to H. J. Holt Ltd.,
Builders' Merchants. In the autobiography he wrote:

I was bound apprentice for four years, beginning at five
shillings a week. They for their part undertook to teach me
the trade of builders' merchant, to which was added ironmongery . . . and many more. I undertook to be punctual,
honest, hardworking, not to swear or seduce my master's
daughter, etc. All this printed on a form with blanks for
my name and theirs, and a six-penny stamp.

After Holt's, Hopkins worked for three other builders'
merchants during the depression years from 1932 to 1938,
until his departure for London under the circumstances
discussed in Llewelyn Powys' Letter 36 and those following.

Throughout these years Hopkins wrote constantly, his
topics slowly shifting from outdoor to amatory concerns,
although his love lyrics are not wholly house-bound. I
have seen a red school-exercise book from his twelfth
year, inscribed "Poems written by me, H. K. Hopkins, in
1927," which contains fifteen poems, plus a list of the
twenty-five largest African cities and the menu for the
Annual Bike Trip ("dinner—4 fishpaste sandwitches . . . .
tea—4 B&B sandwitches . . . ."). Most are narrative: three
tell of war, three laud England, one is a rallying cry for
his Boy Scout troop,

The 13th is the oldest troop that ever the town has known,
Twas started soon after the seeds, by Baden Powell, were sown,

and eight are yarns of the sea:

> With eyes that gleam in the compass light,
> And face a dull, unateral white,
> He grasps the wheel with frenzied grip,
> Last man alive on that dreadful ship.

Nor is the myth Coleridgean: twelve stanzas later the last man dies.

Deft pencil sketches in the exercise book show the same open-air preoccupations—destroyers, steamers, windjammers, lorries, and switching engines—except for one section just after the center staples where a goodly collection of faces peer out from church pews, suggesting that the artist had moved his pad into the choir loft. Noses are his first concern vis-à-vis the congregation—grotesqueries of all sizes and turnings—although Hopkins himself comes well and normally equipped.

(I offer no sampling of the early love poems here: several appear in the correspondence; and the events of the years following his apprenticeship are recounted in the letters.)

After five years with a mobile laundry unit during World War II, Kenneth Hopkins was employed for a while by Bertram Rota, the bookseller, worked on Fleet Street as the literary editor of *Everybody's Weekly,* and wrote voluminously. Since 1954 he has devoted full time to his writing (he lives now in Liss, Hampshire) and to teaching. After a number of lecture trips to American universities, he was given a permanent appointment to the faculty of Southern Illinois University where he is in residence one term each year. He married the Elizabeth of his sonnets in 1939, and their son Edmund, born in 1953, is at Christ's Hospital, Coleridge's and Lamb's school (now in Horsham, Sussex).

What commenced in 1922 with "the Butler, his throat slit," bulks large in the late 1960's with Hopkins in his early fifties—Llewelyn Powys' age when they first met. An updating of Anthony Newnham's *A Check-List of Kenneth Hopkins* (University of Texas, 1961) [1] shows thirty-four entries under his own name, thirteen published pseudonymously, and twenty-five others that he introduced or edited. Among the forty-seven that he wrote are two autobiographical works, five children's books, five books about literature, eight detective novels, ten other volumes of fiction, and seventeen poetic works including *Collected Poems: 1935–1965*—222 poems selected from the sixteen earlier works.

In Hopkins' prose, the substance, the stamina, and the style *sont l'homme*. And in the style an attitude of "let's take nothing in this world with killing seriousness" pervades all his books, no matter what the subject, although it is less conspicuous in the lighter works. *She Died Because . . .* combines detection with buffoonery and literary parody as Dr. Blow, an eighty-one-year-old Doctor of English Emeritus, postpones annotating *Hudibras* in order to elucidate murder. "Clues," he tells his Ralpho, Professor Gideon Manciple, "is the word for what one might call the *apparatus criticus*," and to Detective Sergeant Wix he says, "No need to write all this down, my dear fellow. I've already developed it in a paper read to the Royal Society of Literature; it's in the *Transactions*."

For the most part, Hopkins' pseudonymous works (written cash-and-carry shortly after World War II by "Warwick Mannon," "Arnold Meredith," and "Paul

---

[1] A revised edition was published in 1968 by Southern Illinois University.

Marsh," among others) are novels created "from the motion picture of the same name." The book by "Anton Burney" (#30 in Newnham's *Check-List*) is the most elusive item for Hopkins collectors; its ephemeral nature and suspended distribution account for there being, to my knowledge, but one copy of *The Liberace Story* (London, 1957) in a private collection—Franklin Gilliam's at the Brick Row Book Shop in Houston, Texas. Two of Hopkins' books stem from his 1961 Lectureship at the University of Texas: *A Trip to Texas* (London, 1962), a witty and factual account of his visit, and *Campus Corpse* (London, 1963), which opens with a body and a volume of verse plunging some eighteen stories from the University of Texas Tower.

But it is in his critical books that Hopkins' light touch blends, in a rare way, with his serious thoughts about literature. He is a crusader—a fighter in support of the unread, and against the high priests of esoteric poetry who jealously guard the keys of the kingdom and issue rotund statements. Hopkins writes for the general audience, hoping to cajole, tease, bait, or merely to invite the young and the uninformed to read, and to enjoy. His approach resists brief quotation; here are all his words about *The Ring and The Book* (I have shortened his quotations) in *English Poetry: A Short History* (London, 1963):

> The sense of drama, of history, of men and women human in whatever age and place, which was Browning's strength is consummately and triumphantly employed in his longest poem, *The Ring and The Book*—all twenty-one thousand lines of it. The poem is a study in character: Browning takes the account of a murder case which he finds in an old book picked up on a market-stall, and looks at the affair through the eyes in turn of the general public, the principal protagonists, the lawyers concerned in the case, and the Pope as Judge. To embark upon reading this poem is almost as hazardous an enterprise as taking up *The Faerie Queene* at page one with hopes of arriving safe at the other end; and

comparatively few people these days can steel themselves to attempt either (though they might take courage in the reflection that there is no situation that cannot be worse: it might have been *Aurora Leigh*). Those who do stay the course have been treated to a marathon of psychological insight and some graphic likenesses of types that do not change, whether in seventeenth-century Rome or twentieth-century London. See once more Browning's marvellous power (like Chaucer's) of bringing people alive on the page in a dozen lines:

> I am just seventeen years and five months old,
> And, if I lived one day more, three full weeks;
> 'Tis writ so in the church's register,
> Lorenzo in Lucina, all my names . . . .

This is not portrait- but character-painting; but it brings the girl nearer to us than any parade of detail about the colour of her eyes.

Of Browning's faults there needs to be said very little now. It is true he allowed his exuberance to carry him into some ludicrous uses of language—outrageous rhymes, bits of slang and fustian and pinchbeck (not much of this last, for no honester poet ever wrote) and the best antidote to irritation over these is to read Calverley's masterly parody of *The Ring and the Book,* in which they are all wickedly displayed. Calverley knew Browning's true worth, as any reader may who will approach him without bias; and Calverley's poem ("The Cock and the Bull") like all great parodies serves in the end to confirm the essential greatness of its original. It is a self-indulgence, for quotation is not called for, but I must give myself the pleasure of copying the opening lines, and of taking time from my writing to read the rest; and I hope the reader will be prompted to do the same.

> You see this pebble-stone? It's a thing I bought
> Of a bit of a chit of a boy in the mid o' the day—
> I like to dock the smaller parts-o'-speech,
> As we curtail the already cur-tail'd cur . . . .

Well, that's Calverley's Browning: Browning at his worst; and in some way putting it down in print and reading it over purges the poet of his extravagances, pushes them into a background perspective, and leaves us the freer to enjoy him at his best—and what a rich feast he offers! Landor's noble tribute is not a whit overstated:

> Browning! Since Chaucer was alive and hale,
> No man hath walk'd along our roads with step
> So active, so inquiring eye, or tongue
> So varied in discourse. . . .

The informal manner can annoy (indeed, the *Times Literary Supplement* ignored *English Poetry* when it appeared in 1963, after generous reviews of two earlier books in the same series). But this was Hopkins' prefatory promise:

> Often enough, the emphasis lies more on the small than on the great poets, about whom much has been written already, and about whom the reader will in any case need to read more than can be compressed into a paragraph or a chapter.

> This is not offered as a critical history; it is a plain, unpretentious tale, intended for the general non-specialist reader. . . . It is designed to be such a book as I looked for in vain when, as a lad of sixteen and seventeen, I was discovering poetry for myself, by trial and error.

Alerted by the Preface, perhaps, some critics reviewed the page numbers in the index: Thomas Flatman has more primary pages than Goldsmith, Thomas Haynes Bayly than Crashaw, Samuel Rogers than Rochester, Stephen Duck than Thomas Stearns Eliot, and Sir Richard Blackmore ties with Robert Bridges. But these last two names point, respectively, to two other interests—bad poets and poets laureate. And Kenneth Hopkins has revived the use of the index as bait, rather than crib. The listing for Queen Victoria in *The Poets Laureate* includes: "entirely approves of Wordsworth, 149; receives him in a borrowed suit, 150; told Swinburne is a poet, but is not heard to quote 'Dolores,' 167." (This last tantalizer leads to a footnote that records also the possibility that the laureateship may have gone to Alfred Austin when Lord Salisbury did not distinguish between Swinburne and "Swinford," Austin's manor house.) The following selected index entries are from this book, and from Hopkins' *Portraits in Satire*, a scholarly study of the "silver age of English satire"—Churchill, Anstey, Mason, "The Rolliad," Gifford, "Peter Pindar," and Mathias; in each case the entry stands alone:

Anstey, Rev. Christopher, begets the poet and goes deaf, 77.
Belloc, Hilaire, one of his novels unexpectedly mentioned, 109.
Feeble, Jeremy, not a great figure in literature, 113; quoted, 113.
Longfellow, H. W., a richer poet than Tennyson, 160.
Monmouth, Geoffrey of, an unwitting collaborator with Tate, 45.
Oldfield, Mrs. Anne, is unexpectedly sensible, 71.
Victoria, Queen, just gets in the book, 273n.

Among the books edited by Kenneth Hopkins are *The English Lyric* (Brussels, 1945) ; four volumes in a series described as "A Selection from his Works"—substantial and discerning anthologies from four of his friends, *Edmund Blunden* (1950), *Llewelyn Powys* (1952), *H. M. Tomlinson* (1953), and *Walter de la Mare* (1953) ; and an anthology, *The Worst English Poets* (1958), which is in itself, in part, a consideration of what it is that moves a man to write, or to try to. His interest in the minor poets and in the long line of uneducated poets in England— John Taylor the Water Poet, Stephen Duck, John Jones, John Clare, James Hogg, and others—and his attempts to move larger audiences toward literature are related to his own early urge to write. And always, no matter what tone he chooses, Kenneth Hopkins' enjoyment of literature is as apparent as his wish to share that enjoyment.

3

The Powyses

Seven sons and daughters of the Vicar of Montacute and Mary Cowper Johnson Powys were published authors, and the name of an eighth, the painter Gertrude, appears on title pages as illustrator of her brothers' books. Maurice Hussey's composite bibliography in R. C. Churchill's *The Powys Brothers* (London, 1962) shows a total of 127 entries by the seven—excluding articles in periodicals, contributions to anthologies, and books introduced and edited. When Albert Reginald Powys' name appeared in *Who's Who* in the middle 'thirties, he became the fourth author-brother tapped for contemporary fame. John Cowper and Llewelyn had arrived together in its pages a decade earlier, and Theodore Francis joined them four editions later. And although A. R. Powys' recognition was based mostly on his work as Secretary of the Society for the Protection of Ancient Buildings, his five architectural publications stand high among his qualifications.

The Brontës of Haworth and the Sitwells of Renishaw Hall and London are other examples of more than two writers emerging in the same family in one generation. But few other similarities exist, especially between the convivial, busy life at Montacute Vicarage and the motherless isolation of Haworth Parsonage that turned the Brontës to their own imaginative resources and led them to create their Angria and Gondal worlds far beyond Yorkshire. In a shed behind the kitchen wall, three of the middle Powyses did devise a very private Mabelulu Castle which took its name from theirs—May (Marian), Bertie

(A. R.) , and Lulu (Llewelyn's nickname which his closest friends used throughout his life) . But the only book from Mabelulu is a guest log listing those admitted to their world: "Thomas Hardy—a wayfarer," one entry reads.

The bibliographic truth is that the Powyses were anything but precocious writers: with minor exceptions they did not publish until they had lived into their fifth decade. John, the eldest, produced small volumes of verse in 1896 and 1899—the first when he was twenty-four—but not until he was forty-two did *The War and Culture*, third of his fifty-odd books, appear. Theodore was in print at thirty-three with *An Interpretation of Genesis*—a privately printed pamphlet subsidized by his brother John and Louis Wilkinson—but he too was forty-two when his first full-length book was issued (and forty-eight before the publication of the third of his thirty books, although much of the writing had been done earlier) . Llewelyn's name first appeared on a book when he was thirty-two—over the last ninety pages of *Confessions of Two Brothers*, written with John. He was thirty-nine when *Ebony and Ivory* and *Thirteen Worthies* came out in 1923, although he had been supporting himself through journalism since he was thirty-six. More than two-thirds of the words by the seven Powyses—ninety-two books—appeared after their authors were fifty years old.

Perhaps, as Kenneth Hopkins did with his residences, it is time "to sort out these several" Powyses. Of the eleven children at Montacute, only Eleanor,[1] who died at thirteen, probably of appendicitis, did not reach maturity. Between the eldest, John Cowper (1872–1963), and Theodore Francis (1875–1953) was Littleton Charles

---

[1] Eleanor "could dazzle even her brother John, later to dazzle multitudes," Alyse Gregory has written. "Almost as an infant she took to poetry as a bird to the air." Miss Gregory's warm words for the entire family—the only tribute to consider the Powys daughters—appeared in *London Magazine* in March, 1958.

(1874–1955), long Headmaster of Sherborne Preparatory School and author of two autobiographic volumes. Gertrude (1877–1952), Eleanor (1878–1892), and Albert Reginald (1881–1936) follow. Marian, born in 1882, and for thirty years the owner of the Devonshire Lace Shop, 556 Madison Avenue, New York, wrote an authoritative book in her field, *Lace and Lacemaking* (Boston, 1953). After Llewelyn (1884–1939) was Catharine Edith Philippa (1886–1962), "the poet of our family," Theodore said, and author of the novel *The Blackthorn Winter* (London, 1930). Then William Ernest and Lucy Amelia, the two youngest, born in 1888 and 1890; after the death of her husband, Hounsell Penny, Lucy lived for a time with William on one of his farms near Mount Kenya, but she has returned to Dorsetshire while he remains in Africa.

In so prolific a literary family it is small wonder that Littleton, while preparing his first book for press, proposed to call it *Yet Another*. He had to be dissuaded from using the me-too title by Llewelyn:

> It lacks that "high seriousness" and "style" that Matthew Arnold valued so much. I myself would boldly put down *The Autobiography of Littleton Charles Powys*. . . . Your book is a poetical book and a sound book and deserves better than a clever title.

The eventual title—chosen, like many other Powys titles and character names, after an exchange of letters among the family—reflects what may have been the prevailing mood at Montacute: *The Joy of It*. But biographers are not wholly in agreement about the tenor of life in the Victorian vicarage in Somerset. There are, in fact, such conflicting accounts about the cross-currents of influence and the pressures of personalities at Montacute that it seems desirable to consider the evidence with some thoroughness. Although this book is concerned with writing and not biography, seven writing brothers and sisters is a phenomenon rarely available for study. And the contrast between Llewelyn Powys and Kenneth Hopkins—Kenneth alone of his small family growing up with the urge to write—is important to an understanding of their correspondence.

Antipodal views about life at the Vicarage were held by Littleton Powys and Louis Wilkinson; each had unconcealed prejudices and each rebutted the other, in print and out. In 1937 in *The Joy of It* (the second volume of his memoirs published nineteen years later was *Still the Joy of It*), Littleton gave more details, more homey information about their childhood at Montacute than his brothers in their many autobiographical writings. He told of evenings that "went quickly and happily" with the mother reading to the children and, when they had gone off for bed, to her husband "who tired with the day's work would lie upon the sofa employing his hands in netting—making nets for all sorts of purposes." There were walking expeditions and home-made games and "John would be directing the acting of some play, usually a play of Shakespeare, in which most of the family had parts, and he the most important." Any critic seeking evidence for happiness and permissiveness as nurturers of the creative impulse will find it abundant in Littleton's characterization of his father and mother. Montacute Vicarage, he wrote,

was our home for thirty-two years. And I often wonder whether ever a happier home than ours existed. It was a home of freedom. There were no restrictions except those very lightly placed upon us by our mother who would say: "You must remember the Vicarage is a house set on a hill; you must see that you do nothing to hinder your dear father's work". . . .

Otherwise we could do whatever we liked. Even with our food our freedom of taste was not interfered with; . . . it was never suggested that anyone should eat anything that he or she did not like. . . . [Our mother's] two ambitions were that her children should be happy, and that they should love one another. And the wonderful example that she set of unselfishness, gentleness and love did have the result for which she prayed. For, though in tastes and interests no two members of the family were alike, in affection for each other they were bound together by bonds which nothing in this world could ever loosen. . . .

And our father's character and personality too, went far in the making of this happy home; he was so strong, so independent, so simple, and so consistent; we always knew exactly where we were with him; he gave us a feeling of security such as I have never known since.

Wilkinson's view of the same thing was very different indeed; the psychological tensions that he saw at Montacute would rack all the joy of it. The Powyses appear in four of his books, but that two are catalogued as fiction is not pertinent: *Forth, Beast!* (London, 1946), a continuation of *Swan's Milk* (1934), his "autobiography in the form of a novel," bears this notice: "None of the persons of this book, whether under a real or an invented name, is fictitious; and none of the incidents is fictitious." But *Welsh Ambassadors*, as unabashed biography, is the fairest primary source for his views. On the second page he considers the father, whom he typified elsewhere as one who "invariably sat on his strong-box during his interviews with his lawyer"—Littleton's wife's father. Wilkinson wrote:

It was indeed . . . he that had created, with the unwitting power of some dim prehistoric god, both that "Powys solidarity" in which the identity of each one of his children could be merged, and, no less, the identity of each one of them, so separate, so distinct in all its definitions. My early experiences as a guest at Montacute Vicarage, the only alien at that great Powys Table *surmounted by the Father,* excited and baffled me, disconcerted and embarrassed me. . . .

I was not only nonplussed but resentful; for there seemed something preposterous and unallowable about this great strong thick wall of Powys solidarity, as though it stood there blasphemous against the solidarity of the human race. As "anti-social" as the family motto *Parta Tueri*. . . . I can hear him now, reading prayers or making his own so brief and simple ones, uttering them in his kind, gentle voice, with his look of mild forbearance as though of a Christian head of a Christian family; a voice and look so shockingly belied by the wolf-like implications of his face and the grim resistant *Parta Tueri* line of his mouth. . . .

No talk, indeed, could have been simpler than that of the Powys dinner table. The father rarely used words of more than three syllables, and he preferred those of one or two. He did not know many others, nor did he wish to know them. Any language but the simplest was to him an object of suspicion and contempt. . . .

Mrs. Powys was friendly to me, well disposed; even, in her shy way, affectionate: chiefly, I thought, because she saw me shy and subdued. If she had seen me gay and self-assured I doubt if she would have liked me at all. She was a romantic, sensitive, melancholy and morbid woman, indeed of William Cowper's blood. It was her qualities that made her children's genius, and the qualities of her children's father that give it power to act, and fused with it the strange cruelty by which it is so often controlled. It needed the mental masochism of the mother, the repressed ferocity of the father, to produce *Wolf Solent . . . Unclay . . . Black Laughter*.

Later in *Welsh Ambassadors* Wilkinson revealed that he had first written: "It needed the mental masochism of the mother and the repressed sadism of the father." Llewelyn Powys objected. "He said that his father was not a sadist . . . and in deference to the convinced opinion of a son, I altered 'sadism' to 'ferocity.'" (In a later letter to Wilkinson Llewelyn wrote, "I think he had very little cruelty in him. His outbursts were always the outbursts of a herbivora—a buffalo's fury, rather than the leopard's malice. He was, I swear to you, essentially a grass eater.") Wilkinson went on, in *Welsh Ambassadors*, about the genius of the brothers:

And it needed the blood of John Donne as well. Reading Theodore's and Llewelyn's books, and John's, I am never for long unconscious of the hereditary influences of Donne and Cowper, determining, as I think, so much of their romantic excess, their melancholy, their obsessions, their disease and their madness.

The fact is, to take the lesser point first, that most biographers—perhaps following the lead of this best friend of the family—have allowed their creative imaginations or wishful thinking to dominate their common sense in describing the Powys ties with William Cowper and John Donne—have even perhaps, in loosely using familiar words like *ancestor, descendant, family tree, bloodline* as points of interpretive departure, succumbed to what might be termed *le vice anglais biographique*. Many thousands of Englishmen could trace comparable genealogies: the Powyses' maternal great-grandfather was the Reverend John Johnson, whose grandfather was a brother of Cowper's mother. Johnson is the "Johnny of Norfolk" of Cowper's *Letters* who, after Mrs. Unwin's illness and death, cared for his aging second cousin. Wilkinson's "blood of John Donne" is an even more tenuous connection. Reference in Cowper's correspondence to "our venerable ancestor, the Dean of St. Paul's," suggests that he thought himself in a direct line, but William Cowper's maternal great-great-grandfather, Thomas Donne (1615–1685) was not one of John and Ann Donne's dozen. The rootstock, however, may well have been the same; born just one hundred years after Donne's death, Cowper probably drew on some family knowledge in making the connection.

But *Welsh Ambassadors* has more to say of Mary Cowper Johnson Powys:

Mrs. Powys hated success. She hated, with secret intensity, well-constituted people, or even people whose health was too good. When Llewelyn developed consumption and was determined not to die of it, she was far from friendly to his insistent will. She did not like his going to Switzerland, she did not like him having so many windows open. "These young men," she said, "seem to want to live for ever." . . . If Llewelyn had been content to die uncomplainingly at Montacute Vicarage, without a struggle, his mother might have loved him best of all.

In a late chapter of *The Joy of It*, Littleton directly attacked Wilkinson—or Louis Marlow, the name he used on *Welsh Ambassadors*:

I resented very much the picture he drew of my father and mother. He was only introduced to Montacute in the later years of our home life there, and the few occasions he stayed there, when both my parents were ageing and the family was largely scattered, scarcely justified him in taking upon himself to be the interpreter of the family as a whole. The technical words of psycho-analysis always bother me; they are commonly used so ignorantly and so affectedly. Louis Marlow, I grant, is not ignorant, he knows the full meaning of the words he uses. And when I found my father, one of the most simple-minded, the most kind and the most honest of men called a sadist, and my mother, of all women one of the most spiritual, the most liberal and the most gentle, called a masochist, I must confess I had some difficulty in restraining my feelings towards this writer. He had done this so as to be able to show how my brothers John, Theodore and Llewelyn, than whom no men on earth are more gentle and less cruel, have derived their sadistic tendencies; which he says are so clearly demonstrated in their writings. All I can say is that if they have these tendencies, no human being on this earth is without them, so why make so much of them? My brothers are most painfully aware of cruelty, it is hateful to them, and they hope by showing it in all its hideousness to make the horror of it more universal.

"What a life we had, what a rare happy life, in that old rambling early Victorian Vicarage!" John burst out in the fourth chapter of his *Autobiography* (New York, 1934), and as early as the fifth page of nearly six hundred he denies the existence of sadism in his father. The holograph in the Colgate University Library shows heavy, circular cancellations at this point—and a marginal notation asks "describe father?" in this section—but if the corrections are a bit more frequent here, the difficulty may well have been that of getting started; recovery of the cancellations discloses only changes in diction, not changes of mind. The finished copy reads:

> My father must have been totally devoid of the least trace of sadism—that aberration of which I was doomed as I grew older to become so fatally familiar—for the only way he ever punished us, me and my two brothers, was by suddenly and without a second's warning, giving us one single box on the ear.

John was himself preoccupied with sadism, with the *idea* of it, and a casual reader may overlook a buried fact—buried, that is, by an author whose literary vice is iteration, but who says this only once:

> I only *practiced* sadism about three times in all my days; on those worms in the Northwold Summer-House, on those newly-hatched little birds in the Sherborne quarry,—and even of that incident I am doubtful—and on those beetles I once killed at Rothesay House with scalding water. Never has any cerebral vice been as exacting, as exclusive, as limited in its scope, as mine.

Of his father he wrote:

> I sometimes think that no one who has ever lived has had intenser moments of happiness in life than my Father. . . . he seemed to have a power of enjoyment . . . double that of ordinary human beings. . . . Since his pride and his reserve hindered him from displaying this emotion in public, he hardly ever started down that Vicarage drive, to set out upon one of those parochial excursions which were an excuse for the long walks he loved, without at some moment—between the front door and drive gate—quickening his steps

in this silent ecstasy which was his worship of life. This is really . . . what his eleven children owe to him: the power of falling into an ungovernable transport, in the midst of the most ordinary things.

Marian Powys Grey's memories of childhood at Montacute are happy ones, and she too stresses, in a letter written in 1965, the freedom and the constant reading that impressed Littleton:

> As children we all had a great freedom. We could read, think, and do all we wanted. Our mother would read aloud all the evening in the drawing room.—First to the little ones from the nursery, then the older ones and then every evening always to our Father till he went to bed—and then she would draw near the fire and open her own book to read to herself.
>
> In the afternoon when sitting up to the diningroom table, mending and darning, she would have her book open in front up against the big work basket. I think she was the inspiration to us all.

Mrs. Grey goes back further, however; in conversation recently she traced her mother's love for reading to the influence of her governess—who was Louis Wilkinson's mother.

Llewelyn Powys reacted less vocally to the broad questions of psychotic tensions—or lack of them. He stood between John Cowper and Louis Wilkinson on many counts; and "my father's fifth son" (as John often referred to him) felt conflicting influences from the eldest and the second eldest of the eleven, a fact Littleton recognized in *The Joy of It*. "My efforts were all in vain," Littleton said of his attempts to interest his younger brothers in cricket, a game in which he was himself a west-country star for many years. "They all followed in the steps of John who hated it." But it was a different matter with football:

> Llewelyn as a young boy had the making of a really good

forward, but unfortunately he never grew big enough. He strove to excel at it, spending hours dribbling the ball up and down. . . . In those days I was his hero brother; his devotion to me was wonderful. But later his growing love of literature became so strong that he largely lost his interest in games, and sat at the feet of his brother John whose knowledge of literature and originality of mind fascinated him. And now when I read his noncontroversial writings I feel that at any rate the literature of the Country has been benefited by his change of loyalties at that time.

And Llewelyn's more balanced reaction came too from his fuller sense of realism. When Louis Wilkinson asked permission to quote, in *Welsh Ambassadors,* from the letters Llewelyn had written to him, Llewelyn answered:

It would please me to look over these God damned letters that you propose to print—and then I would be able to judge better. I do not think I am likely to give you much trouble, but in such matters one is apt to be sensitive where least expected. With regard to the Black Woman I do not imagine you will find me touchy on this score. It depends of course on the style of the letter. . . .

Send me a batch of the letters you want to quote and I will cast my eye over them—indicating any passage that I *would prefer* to have left out. I don't suppose I will be at all touchy. For if you are a dry dog-turd it is no use pretending you are not a dry dog-turd, or so it seems to me now on July 23rd.

Llewelyn quoted often, as one of his maxims, the oracular line that Montaigne had engraved on the ceiling of his tower room:

The for and the against, both are possible.

But binary answers oversimplify too, as Llewelyn said in various ways, and as John pointed out to Malcolm Elwin, in a letter discussing the decision to open Llewelyn's files, five years after his death:

I have no fear over a life of Lulu *except one alone,* namely
that it will, for one reason or another reason or for *no*
reason but just liking the dull & safe, draw back from repre-
senting him as—well! I was going to say "as he was"—but
of course we are all of us so very different according to the
person we're with—all chameleons, and Lulu undoubtedly. . . .

But I *say!* these things, I mean the thin pieces of ice in a
family like ours, are awfully ticklish touch mumpy explosive
pieces of Synthetic Ice. . . . You see of course there's Lulu
to me—Lulu to you—Lulu to ——, to ——, to ——, to
——.[1] At least a dozen Lulus, & then finally there's Lulu
to Lulu. And why so explosive ice? because of Lulu's
peculiar attraction—simply *that!*—& the fact that he is *her*
attraction, *my* attraction, *your* attraction, and so on! How
is a Biographer to go to work? eh?

The letter about the assignation with the Black Woman
("she laughed a delicious catlike laugh all the time") in
Welsh Ambassadors brought one fraternal protest. Llewelyn answered Littleton:

I would first wish to say that though there are matters in
those letters that were never meant for publication and
make me feel foolish, I experience no kind of disquietude
about the amorous exploits of my youth and would prefer
them to be known rather than not known and do not at all
object to scaring away conventional people. I think more
good is done by such frankness than harm. . . . For example,
amongst my own friends you would find that "the gentry"
and the "lower classes" would be amused rather than
shocked . . . and this would be the case in China, in Asia, in
Africa, every place in fact which was concerned with no
ambition for preserving intact some particular field for provincial social operations. For example, Dr. —— would be
shocked and Dr. ——, H—— the clergyman, Miss ——,[1] . . .
but Wyndham Goodden, Delemare [an African friend],
Cole, old Weld, Jack, Willie, Dreiser, Massingham, Pollock,
Freud, Lady Warwick, Theodore, Bertie, Gertrude, Jules

---

[1] The names were omitted by Louis Wilkinson, who edited the published letters of John Cowper and Llewelyn.

Romains, Marian, Ralph, the Sitwells, Bernie, indeed about all men-of-letters except perhaps T. S. Eliot[2] would have minds that take for granted that a wide allowance should be made for all matters of sex, *a kind of plenary indulgence,* and this was the old classical attitude, and a very good one too and still recognized amongst intelligent people in London, Paris, Vienna, Pekin, San Francisco. I owe Louis Wilkinson a very great service in clearing my mind as yet a boy of a great deal of what Montaigne used to say was *inconvenient* to conversation amongst intelligent people.

When *The Joy of It* came out the following year, Llewelyn wrote to Littleton:

I am very glad you reproduced that idyllic photograph of Mother and Father. It appears very well opposite your words refuting the views of Louis. Actually I cannot say I like this photograph, nor do I think these shadows of a conventional ideal approach the reality of these two remarkable ones. I can't bear that sugar-sweet, unintellectual smile on Mother's face, nor the old clergyman mask of Father's countenance. If you cover up Mother's mouth then only are you once more aware of the strange passionate power and beauty of her personality so far removed from the Victorian image that will be welcomed by the general public. But I am glad it is published because it does present a side which up to now had not been shown. . . .

P.S. You must not misunderstand my *personal* reaction to this ideal orchard photograph. I am glad you published it. It represents one true side of Mother and Father but in my opinion a side without real significance. Father was a great deal more than the simple old-fashioned English clergyman

---

[2] East Coker, ironically enough, is five miles east and south of Montacute; there are few terser antitheses to Llewelyn's beliefs than "In my end is my beginning," or these lines from Part II of Eliot's *East Coker:*

Shall I say it again? In order to arrive there,
To arrive where you are, to get from where you are not,
  You must go by a way wherein there is no ecstasy.
In order to arrive at what you do not know
  You must go by a way which is the way of ignorance.

suggested by this picture. Below his coat was the shy original unworldly poetical-natured man so well described by John, *who would not easily be duplicated.* . . . My whole nature repudiates this pretty simpering Darby-Joan picture of the mother who read to me *Tom Jones, Tristram Shandy,* the *Autobiography of Benvenuto Cellini,* and was so entirely separated from the ordinary middle-class mother of the orthodox type.

In the "imaginary autobiography" *Love and Death* Llewelyn told of his father's anguish following the death of Mrs. Powys, told of finding his father gardening in August, and weeping: "Indeed, the roughed-up gravel-mould was wet with tears that had been steadily falling from the eyes of this proud old man of countless inarticulate reserves whom not one of us had ever known to cry." When the son, his heart yearning with sympathy, asked "What is it?" the old man's words came at last. "There is nobody now to come and see what I do!" The clash and union of these two—and the give and take of Vicarage life—fashioned eleven children and seven writers, three of them masters.

4

The Ailing Author

Happiest of the Powyses born rapidly to the Vicar and his wife was Llewelyn. The eldest, John Cowper, eleven when this eighth child arrived, remembered holding him "before his baby skull had closed"; and of Llewelyn as a toddler he said, "I can see his face now, . . . like 'the angel that John saw in the Sun.'" In *The Joy of It* Littleton, the second son, called Lulu "the most sunny, happy, winning small boy it was ever my lot to see." Malcolm Elwin's *Life* tells that Llewelyn, waiting to be measured for a velvet suit at age four, "was so excited at being alive that his mother had to be called to stop his jumping up and down and repeating, 'Happy me! Happy me!'" And Llewelyn himself wrote that "the sense of existence would suddenly fill me with exultation so that I could have lifted up my head and crowed like a cock a dozen times in the day."

> All life was then a pleasure. It was a pleasure to have the lessons interrupted by my mother coming in to look after her tame white dove strutting over the sandy floor of its roomy cage with its pink feet. It was a pleasure to learn the poem Wordsworth wrote to a kitten playing with leaves, or the poem by William Allingham that begins "Up the airy mountains". . . .

At age eleven he first left the Vicarage, but only to travel nine miles east, to Sherborne Preparatory School. Llewelyn wept on his departure, but his first letter home, the week after, showed little of the unhappiness that plagued John's early school years, and none of the misery that forced Theodore to withdraw shortly after arriving at Sherborne:

September, 1895   Acriman House, Sherborn

My dear Mother I hope you are all well I saw pupy Yesterday. I hop my speling is not so very bad, love to Emily tell Willy he must behave himself and not bother you love to May and to the Mabelulu how are the tunips geting on we play hocey and cricet I am going to go to the Lyons [Harry Lyon was one of John Cowper's best friends; in 1896 John married his sister, Margaret Alice Lyon] to diner today. I am so loing to go home this establishmend is not so very bad I saw Wrothy the day bifor yesterday he is kind you can tauk to him like I can to Berty tell tom [Littleton] that I have see Berny in Tufins there are a few nise chapes at the prep now but not many I remain youre loving son

Llewelyn Powys

At nineteen, arriving at Cambridge, as the *Life* tells, "escorted by his father to Corpus, the college where he had been preceded, not only by his father and his brothers John and Littleton, but by both his paternal and maternal grandfathers, [he] was allotted the same spacious panelled room . . . as John had occupied a dozen years before." Soon Llewelyn sought out Louis Wilkinson, despite John's and Theodore's belief that they had "better not" introduce their young brother to the "Archangel"—Theodore's ironic tag for the young man who had corresponded with Oscar Wilde, and been sent down from Oxford for staging a mock mass. In *Swan's Milk* Wilkinson recorded "Louis Marlow's" early impressions of Llewelyn:

Nearly all of the many Powyses have charm, but Llewelyn abounds in it incomparably. His smile alone, with its broad sudden light, is enough to win the stoniest heart. So is that air of woodland simplicity and artlessness, which he still can wear, although he is now [1934] as full of guile as the craftiest of all those animals that his writings have invoked for metaphor or simile. . . . The young Llewelyn, with his crisp curly bright hair and fair complexion, had a sunlike look; he was dazzlingly bright. He had light eyes, eager and easily troubled, a rich unguarded mouth, a child's soft mouth greedy of pleasure and sometimes sulky. His body was hard and slight, with a hint of frailness, though one could not, then, have anticipated that he was to be so soon consumptive. . . . He had an unusually large head which seemed even larger than it was because of its stiff woolly growth of light gold curls.

Images of the sun, life-giving and Apollonian, appear from the very first descriptions of Llewelyn, long before he adopted the symbol of sun and life, the phallic ankh, as the colophon for his books. But the sun is the common friend of youth, as gamboling and jumping up and down are the normal exuberancies of healthy young animals. Llewelyn Powys brought about the miracle of carrying over to maturity his joy in being alive. Here, child's glee fathered a slower deeper joy. John chose well an epitaph for his "father's fifth son"—"A loving heart is hard to quench."

It is perhaps only human nature to seek flaws in the psychic armor of a writer who holds what may be minority views—who may seem a dangerous crank—who proclaims his atheism and preaches his hedonism. But there is such consistency in all of Llewelyn Powys' thirty-odd books that the reader comes first to find the armor chinkless and then to realize that there is no armor, but the whole man himself. And the sun continued to be the image for Llewelyn. In her Introduction to the *Letters,* Alyse Gregory described a stranger's reactions on meeting her husband:

I remember an occasion when we went to visit a cottage woman at Montacute who was dying, and as he leaned down over her she cried out in a transport: "Why, it is the sun!"

When we were living at Patchin Place [1922–1924] he used
to come to meet me in the afternoon as I returned from
my work, and I recall how his figure seemed suddenly to
come up out of the noisy Seventh Avenue pavement with
all summer in his face.

There is irony in his contracting, while still a young
man, the one disease for which the sun was then thought
most therapeutic. After his "three riotous years" at Cambridge—he was ploughed in the History Tripos in June,
1906, but passed, with a second class, five months later—
Llewelyn tried teaching at three schools, lecturing in
America with his brother John, private tutoring, and
"writing for the papers," although he did not then put
writing to the total test. The Reverend Charles Francis
Powys allowed his single sons £60 a year, the married sons
£100; Theodore, married and living in Chaldon Herring,
succeeded in living on his allowance (except for one brief
school-lecture interval) until he was forty-eight and began
to derive some income from his writing. In the spring,
1908, Llewelyn proposed "to get Theodore to lend me his
back room. I shall . . . read all the evenings . . . and labour
in the mornings and afternoons. . . . I mean to work
frantically, desperately—sending articles and scraps again
and again to the various editors." The idea had not yet
passed "that invaluable second chamber that we Powyses
consult at Montacute," but if the plan found favor with
Father, "which I'm afraid is unlikely, . . . I am going to
make one last great effort to get out of this horrible profession . . . one last effort to dodge the blackboard."
    There is no record of what happened in the "second
chamber" but within a short time Llewelyn began preparing a series of lectures similar to those that John had
been giving in America for the three years past. But unlike John—who was for more than a quarter of a century
one of the most spectacular performers on the lecture
circuit—and unlike Louis Wilkinson—whose American lec-

tures brought him an honorary doctorate from St. John's College, Annapolis—Llewelyn was not a success. Wilkinson reported that Llewelyn's earliest attempt, in New York City, December, 1908, was "one of the most acutely embarrassing and distressing experiences I ever had." Wilkinson described his embarrassment in *Welsh Ambassadors:*

> He stammered, paused, stammered again: one after another of his sentences crumbled and fell to pieces, and then, for many moments together, he would be, it seemed, struck dumb. He had notes; indeed, I think he had the whole lecture written out, but he was trying not to use the manuscript, and when he did in desperation fall back on it, it completely bewildered him. After the lecture, questions had been invited. Llewelyn was asked what he thought of some novel of Meredith's. Terror-stricken—for he had not read that novel—he was silent for a while, then with immensely solemn emphasis he replied: "I think—what *I* think is—*I* think it's a—a very—a *very good book.*"

> After the lecture I went back with him to our lodgings and slept with him there. He was in extreme agitation, in real misery and despair. He could hardly speak. When he was undressed, his whole body seemed, most singularly, to exude his anguish and dismay. It put me in mind of the agony and bloody sweat in the garden of Gethsemane. He had exaggerated, fantastically and beyond all measure, that evening's misadventure. . . . This is a Powys characteristic . . . to be disquieted by chimeras.

With practice Llewelyn improved, Wilkinson said, "but he never took to it," and with the conclusion of the three-month tour came a series of what might be called triumphant disengagements. "Free at last!" he had written in his diary on giving up private tutoring at Calne in August, 1908, and in March, 1909, on the day of his last American lecture he wrote, "Finished in Glory—Free." In June, after serving as an assistant master for Littleton at Sherborne for six weeks, he wrote "Finished in Glory—Free," and left with his youngest brother, Willie, for *Lorna Doone* country in Devon. They "walked over Dunkery and down by Badgworthy Water," and had supper at John Ridd's farm, but then John Cowper was reported ill in London and they broke off their holiday. The next month, after helping to nurse his brother back to health from one of his recurrent gastric attacks, Llewelyn wrote, "Jack is free —Finished in Glory."

But Llewelyn was neither free—nor settled. He rejected repeated chances to become a junior director in the publishing house of William Rider and Son (Ralph Shirley, his cousin, held a controlling interest in it) because he could not bring himself to face regular hours and routines; and, while still exploring the possibility of returning to American lecturing, he accepted Littleton's offer to re-engage him at Sherborne. The diary excerpts for the fall, 1909, record the normal activities of an assistant master until—abruptly—the entry for Wednesday, November 3, is "in bolder handwriting."

> There is blood in my mouth. That drop of blood is my death warrant; I must die.

Welsh Ambassadors puts the last sentence in quotation marks; Elwin's scrupulously accurate *Life* does not. But Llewelyn Powys was not borrowing subconsciously: he knew the literary source as well as he knew "the colour of that blood."

Powys has told in detail the story of the consumption he lived with for the next thirty years—in *Confessions of Two Brothers, Skin for Skin, Verdict of Bridlegoose, Earth Memories*. In fact, no one of his books, including *Henry Hudson,* is wholly free of autobiography.

The next month John took him to Clavadel Sanatorium at Davos Platz, where he stayed for nearly two years. In 1912, after a foolhardy leap-day trek alone from Arosa over Furka Pass to Frauenkïrch, he suffered a relapse and re-

turned briefly to Davos Platz—leaving, in fact, seven weeks
before Thomas Mann arrived with his sick wife. But while
Mann was first viewing the axis of the valley at Davos
Platz, Llewelyn was with John and Louis, on Louis'
honeymoon, in Venice. That fall Llewelyn was again ill,
but—despite running a temperature often—there were no
serious recurrences until the summer, 1924. Then, soon
after returning from a camping trip through the Rocky
Mountains with Dr. James Sibley Watson, Jr., of *The
Dial,* he had a hemorrhage on a train while going to visit
Alyse Gregory's parents in Norwalk, Connecticut. Sporadic
attacks followed—at Palestine, in Capri, at home in Dorset—until August 4, 1933. The terse entry for that day in
Malcolm Elwin's chonology in the *Life,* speaks for the last
six years of his life:

> Serious haemorrhage resulting from sun-bathing and hence-
> forth an invalid.

A few weeks before his death, the editors of *Twentieth
Century Authors* (New York, 1942) received from Llewelyn Powys a résumé of his life. Although some of the
facts are given above and some of his details seem selected
for an American audience, I quote it in full so that his
omissions can be as apparent as the things he chose to
emphasize:

> I was the eighth child of the Rev. Charles Francis Powys
> and Mary Cowper (Johnson) Powys. My father was the
> grandson of Littleton Powys, the only brother of the first
> Baron Lilford. The Powys family is of Welsh extraction, but
> has been settled in England since the sixteenth century. My
> mother's grandfather was the poet Cowper's first cousin. I
> was educated at Sherborne School, and at Corpus Christi
> College, Cambridge, taking my degree in 1906. In the spring
> of 1909 I lectured in America on English literature under
> the auspices of the University Extension Society, and at a
> Whitman anniversary had the honour of reciting "When

Lilacs Last in the Dooryard Bloomed" from the same platform from which Professor Woodrow Wilson also gave an address.

On my return to England I fell sick with consumption and spent two years at Clavadel in Switzerland. In 1914 I sailed to British East Africa, spending five years as manager of a stock ranch belonging to the Hon. Galbraith Cole. After a year spent in England I returned once again to the United States and began at the age of thirty-six to earn my living by writing. The publication of *Ebony and Ivory* by Mr. Simon Gould of the American Library Service brought me some reputation that was soon strengthened by the appearance of *Black Laughter* and *Henry Hudson*.

In the year 1925 I returned to Dorset in England with my American wife, Alyse Gregory, who had been managing editor of the *Dial*. For five years we lived in a Coast Guard cottage on the top of White Nose, one of the highest sea cliffs of the South coast, afterwards moving a little inland, where we still rent the same cottage [the rent was fifty dollars a year when they moved in, in 1931]. A recrudescence of my old disorder compelled me in 1936 to return once more to Clavadel in Switzerland, where I am now living.

The chief literary influences that have gone to mould my thought and style are Montaigne, Lucretius, Shakespeare, Robert Burton, Charles Lamb, Walter Pater, Thomas Hardy, Guy de Maupassant, and Marcel Proust. Of the contemporaries I have met I have been most influenced by Sigmund Freud, Theodore Dreiser, Edna St. Vincent Millay, Louis U. Wilkinson, and Thomas Hardy. My political convictions follow those of President Franklin D. Roosevelt, whom I consider the most spirited, the most generous, and the wisest statesman that the world has seen for many years. I hate tyranny of any kind whether it comes from the right or the left. I believe that the pleasures of private property are too universal to be happily abolished. In matters of religion I am a confirmed skeptic. I believe that there exists no conscious principle concerned with man and his affairs. At the back of life all is mystery. I believe that the best clue to life is to be found in the poetic vision and that no purpose of life is of more consequence to the individual than love.

One page is an impossible container for fifty-five years, of course, but these words and all his life and all his works— including the letters to Kenneth Hopkins—afford ample refutation of the idea that serenity cannot generate art.

The articles of Powys' life raise questions about the relationship between physical health and creativity. The best short essay on the complex subject is probably still Hermann Weigand's chapter, "Disease," in his study of *Der Zauberberg* (New York, 1933), and Mann himself considers the phenomenon of *Steigerung* in a January, 1953, article in *Atlantic Monthly*. Most of Llewelyn's writing was done in the "flatlands," but in "A Consumptive's Diary" in *Confessions of Two Brothers*, he said, "my illness had sharpened my wits." Louis Wilkinson, writing twenty years later, said that the disease had "intensified all his perceptions" and heightened "his sense of life's value." Even granting the doubtful premises that fever quickens sensory perception—and that an artist in danger of losing his life values it more highly than another sick man—Powys' tuberculosis was not a major factor in making his philosophy, but only in solidifying it. Several times he wrote of his early realization that there was but one life—that he had found, before going to Cambridge, an answer for his youthful *ubi sunt* questions. "They"—the snows and all dead ladies—"have been drawn back into the secret residua of matter." "At our death," he wrote, also in *Glory of Life*, "the mind is utterly extinguished as is the flame of a farthing dip." The change that came in 1909 is told in *Skin for Skin:*

It seemed to me, during these first hours of my sickness, as though I had done nothing with my life, as though I had been guilty of allowing a priceless opportunity to pass by with the obtuseness of a veritable dizzard. . . . Never again would I suffer myself to be submerged by the commonplace.

The diary excerpts quoted in *Welsh Ambassadors* make his first reactions to illness seem dramatic, but none can accuse Powys (or Keats) of self-dramatization who has not experienced the discovery of a disease whose outcome, then, was more often death than recovery. Llewelyn sketched a tombstone in the diary with his death date tooled in as December 1, 1909—four weeks away. "Father arrives. Yesterday Father sat by my bed side. I cried because Littleton cried: Father prayed—and I looked far away. . . ." Marian came. His mother came. "I have lived twenty-five years, and can cry *vixi*—there is no sensation unknown to me—I have experienced everything." John came and sat by the bed. "At last I find someone who loves as I do—curse!" The parents were not immediately convinced of the wisdom of sending him to Switzerland— a fact that may bear on Wilkinson's attitude toward them —but John insisted and "Father bends his will. . . . His prayers and religion seemed to me very grotesque but his love is very precious." Willie came, Gertrude came, Bertie arrived. "Advent of Archangel. He sits with me all day, we laugh and talk together. I have had some wild dreams— stood at a corner of the street of the city of dreadful night, shouting out "I have been spitting blood blood Blood." Theodore came. "He loves me more than I had thought. *'Primum vivere, deinde philosophari.'* "

Within a short time after arriving in Switzerland, the "temperature down" entries start. And then, in February, 1910, Llewelyn wrote in his diary:

The art of living is to be fully aware of one's personal existence.

This philosophy did not change throughout his life, but another experience five years later—an experience that lasted for five years—reaffirmed all he believed. Whether the African years were needed to strengthen his convictions is problematic, for the gross and garish workings of insensate equatorial nature differed only in degree from weasel and rabbit engagements in Somerset and taloned owls seizing barn swallows in Dorset. But in the land of the Mau and the Kikuyus nature went her way more openly with men, and assailed the senses more strongly. Llewelyn smelled manflesh burning; and kissed "her ebony body—the smell of it was excellent, like the interior of some old and precious box found in the Sultan's attic at Zanzibar." Green parrots screamed overhead. "Willie shot a white-breasted hawk. It lay on the verandah in its death agony. I skinned it—Christ, what eyeballs. Read *Troilus and Cressida.*" He watched leopards mating "and noted the savage sadism displayed by the male. Every time the male had an ecstasy he snarled and bit." One day in March, 1915, he had a visitor; his letter to Wilkinson gave no surname, but certainly it was Baroness Blixen—Isak Dinesen:

I wonder how you would contemplate existence with no one to talk to, no one to have. Sometimes a week passes and I see no one—only these black men who are many of them jolly fellows. . . . One day, it is true, a very attractive figure stepped out of a little mule carriage—a Danish lady, a Baroness—she was on her way to shoot lions and came to me for lunch. She was dressed as Frances was when I first met her, only one of her boy's stockings had a hole in it. She continually reminded me of Frances [Wilkinson's first wife, of the Venice honeymoon]. A very faint delicious sort of scent came from her body—half artificial and half woman. She told me she read Nietzsche as a girl at Elsinore and she also rouged when she went into my room to wash her hands. I do not possess a piss pot so arranged a small basin with exquisite care, but she was too nice for that. Her courier, a Danish officer of no consequence, told me in an awed whisper that she was related to Queen Alexandra.

Powys' sputum was still infected. "Still slight temperature. I am breaking in a colt." He nursed a pet monkey for days, but it died. "Saw a monkey with a brilliant rainbow coloured bottom and the most foul and indecent manners. . . . The Pox is so extraordinarily prevalent." He found that the natives were wholly fatalistic:

> They lose a leg . . . or one of them is eaten up, and they say "Shawi Muga" or "God's affair." They make no effort to avoid disaster, they know if it is to come, it is to come, and perhaps in that they are wise.

In Africa Llewelyn wrote his portion of *Confessions of Two Brothers,* but it was not until 1923 that his first full-length book, *Ebony and Ivory,* was published. There is truth in John Cowper's statement in his introduction to Llewelyn's *Baker's Dozen* (this excellent eight-page commentary appears only in the English edition of 1941) that his brother "needed the real life of something or somebody to set his imagination free," but the more important point relates to his philosophy of life: Llewelyn found it early and maintained it firmly through all his years. Whether his answer was right matters less to his writing than that he was sure *in his own mind.* His certainty brought neither smug complacency nor arrogant fanaticism, but an ardent, atheistical peace of mind. (All who resist the juxtaposing of these five words will be troubled by Powys' works.) And if he ever doubted his answer, there was powerful buttressing from those men he wrote of in *Thirteen Worthies, Rats in the Sacristy,* and *Damnable Opinions* from Akhenaton and Aristippus and Lucretius to Thomas Hardy.

Llewelyn Powys, his five senses perhaps no keener because of a sporadic fever but certainly sharpened by a constant awareness that his days were more meagerly numbered than those of his healthy peers, found too much all about him to squander time on imaginings. Even his two novels are hardly fictitious, and when he tried to fabricate, as in the hurried conclusion of *Apples Be Ripe,* bad writing resulted. And by an easy paradox Powys' writings, so largely autobiographic, are among the least egocentric of this century. His is the one seeing eye in his tales and essays, but, because as viewer he knows precisely where he stands, he is the more objective about his perceptions. Securely centered, he finds little need to set something of himself apart, to report how the object affects him. By the same token, his empathic sense is more highly developed as he is freed from introspective questioning.

Powys was willing to put his beliefs into action. Pain, he held with Epicurus and his followers, was the first evil, and he was as anxious to fight the inflicters of pain as the most zealous moral reformer was to fight the dispensation of pleasure. "Let no persecuted creature call on us twice," he said in 1931 in *Impassioned Clay,* and in 1934 when he heard shocking accounts about the conduct of a nearby home for mentally defective girls, he acted—even though the hemorrhages of the year before had left him a permanent invalid. Malcolm Elwin's *Life* gives the full details of Llewelyn's drafting of a petition asking an investigation, its circulation by James Cobb, a farmer from West Chaldon, and the aid given by his friends Sylvia Townsend Warner and Valentine Ackland—who had themselves, several years earlier when Llewelyn was in America, helped a girl who had escaped from the home. The petition went first to a vicar of the parish (also the "landlord of the property rented by the controllers of the home"), and, when he made no acknowledgment, to a member of the Dorset County Council, where it was again ignored. The quotations from Llewelyn's petition and letters seem reasonable by any humane standards in requesting an impartial investigation, but the Council referred the matter to its own Committee, the one that employed the operators of the home.

The upshot was a libel case brought against Powys, Cobb, Miss Warner, and Miss Ackland—a charge, Elwin indicates, that probably could not have been made "if Llewelyn had taken the precaution to write the words 'Private and Personal' on his letters to the clergyman and the councillor!" The case dragged on into 1935; then a letter from the bed-ridden defendant to Arthur Davidson Ficke in America tells his determination to appear in court two days hence:

> I have set my heart on getting in if I can and am to be carried over the downs in an armchair placed in a dog cart like some —— Buddha for the populace to bawl after and the seagulls to molest. . . . On the village green I am to be met by Mrs. Thomas Hardy's car and conveyed to the Antelope where John . . . will be waiting. The next day, all being well, I shall appear in court. . . . [but] if I see real undiluted blood I shall turn tail wherever I am. For four days I have had discolouration and even a little this morning, but never enough for me to be certain that I could not make the triumphal entry into Dorchester.

On January 18, 1935, in the town of Powys' birth, the four defendants were found guilty. They were fined £100 and costs, each, but Elwin gives the total cost to Llewelyn as £573 8s. 3d.

The libel case had a variety of aftermaths. Llewelyn did not experience poorer health, perhaps, in part, because his philosophy concerned itself with the present, and held no place for self-pity.

He went on writing to the authorities to insure that the promise of continued inspection of the home for mentally defective girls was kept, but now he marked these letters "Personal, Private, and Confidential."

He received, early in March, a letter from Edna St. Vincent Millay:

If you wish to hurt me beyond healing, refuse my gift. I swear to you that I can afford it perfectly well, that I do not need the money; my new book has sold already more than forty thousand copies. But suppose I could not so well afford it, suppose I had meant to use this money for something which now I should be unable to buy—tell me, what could I buy with a thousand dollars so precious as the thought that perhaps I may be helping you to get well? I am ashamed of you, darling. And of Alyse, too. You are both being very naughty.

I know what it is, of course. It is that dingy law-suit, and the Two-Hundred-Pound-Look of Mrs. Nincom and her daughter that have made you two clear beings think about money in this smudgy way. You must both send your wings to the cleaner. . . . [Miss Millay gives her travel plans.]

As for your letters, all about that silly money—as I said in the beginning, if you wish to wound me with a hurt I shall never recover from, persist in this drab madness.

Llewlyn Powys did accept financial aid from several of his friends; he did not possess $3,000.

He was the subject of extensive publicity. VERDICT OF MALICE AGAINST DYING AUTHOR, one headline said, and Elwin tells that "on Sunday, 20th January, double-crown display posters all over England bore the legend, NEWS OF THE WORLD—DYING MAN IN DORSET ASSIZE DRAMA. Another Sunday newspaper, with a circulation of a mere million or so, invited Llewelyn to write an article on the 'Meditations of a Dying Man.'" Powys responded in this vein:

. . . We rely implicitly on the teaching of Epicurus, though it is wise to modify its classical austerity with the fresh dew of natural goodness, of natural heathen compassion. We may disregard the greater part of conventional morality. It has been my experience that gross wickedness has usually been supported by the cowardly acquiescences of a correct society that cares only for the surface appearance of things, and little for the frightened truth that lies hidden behind. As Professor Whitehead has so admirably said: "In all stages of civilization the popular Gods represent the more primitive brutalities of the tribal life. . . ."

The real sins of life are two only—stupidity and cruelty; and against these, without hope of reward, war should be for ever waged by every magnanimous and well-descended spirit. It has long been my steadfast belief that human misery of every kind can in a large measure be lifted through intelligence and generosity. . . .

An assistant ghoul wrote back:

Many thanks for your article. . . . I am afraid, however, that it is not quite what the Editor meant. You have rather flown over the heads of the average reader. . . . I think the article could have been so human and "down to earth" . . . [You could have] stated in absolutely simple language just how you are preparing to meet the end. . . . Are you frightened to die? If you care to try and recast it again on the lines I suggest . . . I will get the Editor to interest himself in it again.

But the newspaper publicity may have had a much more serious effect, Malcolm Elwin suggests:

The gravity of implications from the verdict seems to have occurred neither to lawyers nor the press. The essential point was not whether conditions at the home in question were beyond reproach or otherwise, but the right of ratepayers to demand of their elected representatives investigation of local conditions open to suspicion. At the time of writing [1946], a man has been recently sentenced to six years' penal servitude for causing by cruel treatment the death of a child entrusted to his care as a foster-parent by a local authority. Evidence at the trial disclosed the knowledge of many neighbours that the man was an unfit person to have charge of children. The child's life could have been saved by removal to another home, but nobody was inclined to risk prosecution by laying information against the householder or by demanding official investigation.

In March, 1965, a letter from Sylvia Townsend Warner included these painful words:

> The law of libel is unchanged, so the same thing could happen today.

And—on a happier note—the newspaper publicity may have occasioned the meeting with Kenneth Hopkins. Thirty miles east of Dorchester, the Bournemouth *Daily Echo*'s extensive coverage of the libel case was being read eagerly by an aspiring poet who worked then for Middleton & Co. Ltd., Builders' Merchants.

5

Letters: Chaldon Herring
and Bournemouth
October 30, 1935 to May 31, 1936

KH–1: KENNETH HOPKINS TO LLEWELYN
POWYS[1]

> 125 Southcote Road
> Bournemouth.
> October 30, 1935

Dear Mr. Powys,

I am typing this letter because I would spare you the agony of deciphering my handwriting, and because I feel there is a better chance of beguiling you into reading right to the end.

I suppose I am impertinent to address you at all; at all events, that is nothing to the impertinence I now contemplate, which is no less a thing than inviting myself to call upon you at your home one morning. However, I have some trace of good maners, even if, in my haste, I do omit the second "n"; therefore it is that I warn you of my intention, so that, if the thought of a stranger in your house really appals you beyond bearing you can write and reject my proffered friendship with strange and terrible oaths—and be very sure I shan't blame you.

---

[1] A photograph of this, the only typewritten letter in the correspondence except Hopkins' last to Powys, appears in the illustration section. I have slightly altered the style of Hopkins' heading: the correspondents used a wide variety of formats for return addresses and dates, and I have silently made all uniform. When the date is omitted I record, in square brackets, the information from the postmark on the envelope (all but three were saved) or the postcard. Missing return addresses present no problem: each of the three correspondents made only one thoroughly discussed change of residence during the friendship.

I am a precocious young man of twenty-one, with a higher opinion of my own value as a poet than any man in England, and a vast determination to Make my Mark in Life—and also a vast disinclination to exert myself in furthering this end.

For yourself and your writings I have a great respect, which I mention now because if and when I see you I shall undoubtedly talk of nothing but my own greatness and the superlative excellence of my work (some of which I fear I shall attempt to read, so look out!)

Please allow me to call. Unless I receive definite intimation that the dogs will be loosed at my advent I shall assume that you are prepared to endure my company for half-an-hour; I would probably arrive just after closing time, say twenty-past-two; for the excellence of M/s Strong's bitter would detain me at The Sailor's Return[2] until then.

If you prefer to fix time and date yourself (in order to be sure of being out when I call) please do so, and I will obey

Finally, if I may ask so much, would you acknowledge reciept [ink: ei] of this note, so that I may know you still live at the address to which this is despatched. I should hate to come all that way for nothing, although certainly in those circumstances I should potter up over White Nothe,[3] and take the air; but White Nothe I have seen before, it is yourself I want to see.

---

[2] This pub in Chaldon Herring (the village is also called East Chaldon) was one mile north of Chydyok, Powys' cottage. The landlord's wife, Mrs. Legg, kept one room where visitors to Chydyok sometimes stayed.

[3] In *Dorset Essays* (London, 1935) Llewelyn Powys wrote:

When I first lived in one of the coastguard cottages on the top of the White Nose I was in considerable doubt as to the correct address. As a child I had been taught to refer to the cliff as the White Nore; on the other hand the gate of the coastguard station through which I passed every day presented my eyes with the words White Nothe; while the people of Chaldon Herring were all of them confident that I was living at White Nose. It was this last judgment which eventually won emphatic confirmation from the late Mr. Thomas Hardy, who said: "Of course it is White Nose, it always has been called White Nose. It is like the Duke of Wellington's nose." From that afternoon I have been careful to use the local name. . . . [for] the noblest of all the Dorset headlands.

May I conclude with my good wishes to you, now and always, whether I see you or no?

[S] Kenneth Hopkins
TL.

P.S. Specimen of verse enclosed for your edification, and may I dare to hope—approbation.

The cockiness of this self-invitation—a tone found in no other letters from Hopkins to Powys—is typified by the letters "TL" printed at the end of the line underscoring Hopkins' signature. When he was a young Boy Scout, Kenneth Hopkins has told me, he was given—or perhaps gave himself—the nickname "Tishbite Laureate," a half-nonsense tag chosen as much for the lilt and the sound of the syllables as for the reference to his young poetic bent or prophetic talent. Now, some half a dozen years later, Hopkins' use of the old Scout initials, meaningless to the author he addressed, seems defensive bravado—a preparation for possible rejection—even as the misspelling seems almost deliberately to stand when retyping would have been short matter. (His diary shows that he held the letter two days before posting it, and either dated it ahead of time or added the date before sending it off.) Should Powys' answer be no—or silence—the Bournemouth apprentice can tell himself that it had all been a lark, a spur-of-the-moment letter—or that he expected no answer. But the enclosure certifies that the self-invitation was earnest, that only the method was glib. This was the specimen sent along for Powys' "edification":

O heart be strong, heart that is lonely, sing!
Take lovliness that dies for pattern and guide,
Sing, though none will remember the singer who died;
Sing of romance and love for comforting.
Remember the friends who loved you in their day,
With whom was peace, in whom your trust was laid;
Remember friends that fail, and loves that fade,
And sweet companionships that fled away.

In sorrow there is beauty, and the sleep
Is kindlier than dreams that follows tears;
Music recalls the love of other years,
And faithless friends whom faith was vain to keep.
The crowding memories a song can bring!
Heart that is lonely, heart that is lonely, sing!

* * * * * *

H. K. Hopkins[4]
1935

His intense urge to write—and to succeed at writing—
had been recorded by Kenneth Hopkins earlier in the
week that he wrote to Llewelyn Powys. In the University
of Texas Hopkins Collection is a tall, thirteen-by-eight
ledger, bound in red cloth, its first entry dated 26 October
1935. The title page is meticulously lettered:

POEMS
With Notes
by
H. K. HOPKINS
Bournemouth:
at the home of the author
1935

A two-page Preface sets forth the unemployed author's
purpose: "I propose copying into this volume such of my
verse as seems to me at this time worth saving. The reminder as far as I am concerned can be burnt." The
Preface points out that an unpublished poet has a difficulty
("he is his own public and critic"), and a luxury ("I am
obliged to consult only myself"). For those critics who "in
time to come, reading my verse, may seek its derivations,"
he issued a caveat ("I believe my style, if any, to be

---

[4] This is the only reference in the letters to Hopkins' first name;
poems written in a school exercise book, during his twelfth year,
are signed "Hector, Lord Hopkins."

founded on that of no other poet"), but "to save such critics a certain measure of trouble, here is a list of my 'favourite' poets: J. E. Flecker,[1] H. Belloc, G. K. Chesterton, T. S. Eliot, G. M. Hopkins, W. B. Yeats, E. A. Poe, Herrick, Marlowe, Blake. Let them make what they can of that." But at the same time "I have an appalling ignorance of Chaucer, Spencer, Shakespere, Shelley, Keats, Wordsworth, Byron, Tennyson, and the estimable John Oxenham." The anticlimactic listing of the living author, William Dunkerley, under his pseudonym is among a few jibes at himself in the journal, but for the most part the tone is serious:

> As to my theory of Poetry, or my mission, or my message, or what not, shall I tell it? Firstly, like someone else, I write because I must. Secondly, (hear Flecker on this one:) ". . . if we have preaching to do, in Heaven's name, let us call it a sermon and write it in prose. It is not the poet's business to save man's soul, but to make it worth saving." This volume too "is written with the single intention of creating beauty."

After the Preface, Hopkins transcribed a number of poems, starting with sonnet "Three" of April, 1932. His notes are conversational and self-critical. "Nos. 1 and 2 I have scrapped. . . . Nos. 4 to 9 I have scrapped. The curious may see them in earlier M.S.S., but they are very inferior, in my opinion: I should not wish them to be published, except as curiosities, or in an Appendix to my Works." Hopkins was not hiding his verse, the note on "Twelve" indicates: "This sonnet has called forth more admiration than I think it deserves." Nor was he unwilling to revise:

---

[1] Hopkins might well have noticed in the biographic facts about Llewelyn Powys many similarities to details about the first of his favorites, James Elroy Flecker, who was born in 1884, wrote of lands beyond Europe, had tuberculosis, sought health at Davos Platz—and died there in 1915. (All spellings within quotation marks, as noted in Chapter I, are Hopkins' spellings.)

"To change line 5, so that the infinitive is not split, would, I think, be pedantic. 'It is my fate dearly to love and lose.' No! I don't like it so well. This also was written when I was sixteen." Sonnet "28" bears the notation, "Unlike most of my sonnets, this one gave me a lot of trouble— I suppose I must have written and rewritten it a dozen times, before I arrived at the above result."

Then—suddenly—the young poet announced that it had all been an artifice:

> Sixteen pages of this book having been used for poems, I feel now that its real purpose has been sufficiently disguised from the common reader, and I can now reveal it in its true colours as a book of rambling meditations in verse and prose. I wish I could write a book like Dante's Vita Nuova— but alas! I have no Beatrice. . . .

But there was Clarice:

> She is not pretty, or beautiful, or even attractive. Skinny is the word one might use to describe her. I have never at any time observed the least trace of brain in her skull. But of this I am certain, given the least opportunity, in love with her I would fall! . . .

And there was Muriel:

> She is more intelligent, and also, I suppose, better looking. I like her less, but kiss her more! . . .

But poetry was never far from his mind:

> I have never made a poem about Muriel; when I do, be very sure it will be inserted. I once tried, but it was a failure. . . .

Clarice was more inspiring:

> Several of my poems are written for Clarice. They speak in tones of approbation of the glorious music of her name—do you not think it beautiful? Let me write it again: Clarice. Clarice!

Immediately following this entry in the ledger-journal, but dated three days later, is this bald announcement:

> Yesterday I wrote a letter to the writer Llewelyn Powys, which I shall post tomorrow. I hope he replies.

The other news of October 29 is that "My play, Neptune Triumphant or Black Eyed Jake's Mistake in which Procky plays Neptune is to be produced at Pokesdown next Monday." And, "yesterday I wrote a satirical letter to the editor of the Weekly Post, a rag. Today a reply arrives. —30/10/35. I reply to the Post, chiding them for two spelling mistakes and other inaccuracies." The same day— before mailing it to the Bishop of Winchester—Hopkins transcribed into the diary a threnody, "On the Ven. A. E. Daldy: Died October 29, 1935," the Vicar of St. Peter's, which closed with the lines:

> We thank the living Christ for such as he,
> True Saints whose work endures eternally.

Then came an answer from Chaldon Herring.

AG–1: ALYSE GREGORY TO KENNETH HOPKINS

Chydyok,
Chaldon Herring,
Dorchester, Dorset.
October 31, 1935[1]

---

[1] An American reader, remembering and sharing President Kennedy's perplexity about first-class mail requiring five days to go from Boston to Washington, may wonder at the rapidity of British service in the 1930's. A number of letters in this correspondence were written, posted, received, answered, and the answer posted—all on the same day. And I have seen two exchanges of letters between John Cowper Powys in North Wales and Kenneth Hopkins in London that received this same one-day service. Postmarks (of 1938) confirm the dates on the letters.

Dear Mr. Hopkins,

I am writing for my husband, Mr. Llewelyn Powys, who is too ill to write for himself, having been in bed for more than two years. He is not supposed to receive any callers just now as he is only just recovering from a somewhat alarming increase of his illness. If, however, you would feel it worth your while to come this distance to speak to him for five minutes it would give us both pleasure to meet you but our hours are as capricious as our necessities are re-stricted—two-twenty is an impossible hour. Could you come in the morning between 11:45 and 12:30 or any time in the afternoon after 5:45—or any time in the evening, though I fear for you *that* is an impossible time in so dark and isolated a place.

Sincerely yours,
Alyse Gregory

P.S. Will you address me as Miss Gregory since for profes-sional reasons as well as from preference I have always kept my own name since my marriage.

In his ledger-journal Kenneth Hopkins noted receipt of the letter, and what he knew of Llewelyn Powys:

Mr. Powys reply arrived a day or two since, and I replied stating the day of my visit. He has been so ill that I can see him only for a few minutes. All I have read of his writ-ing is 'Apples be Ripe' and what little else I know of him is culled from J. C. Powys' Autobiography. He seems to be a fine man! I hope he likes me sufficiently for me to see him again. I shall leave with him a few of my poems in a book. He has already one sonnet, "O heart be strong." The following are the first lines of the other poems I shall give him.

He listed nineteen poems—only two of which were among the sixteen "worth saving" the week before. But in truth Hopkins had by this time written several hundred poems, and each time he prepared a collection—as he now did for Powys in a small stapled notebook with embossed wallpaper glued to the cover—he selected poems appropriate to the new recipient.

The journal shows but one other reference to Llewelyn Powys before the trip to Chydyok:

> 3 November 35[1]
>
> I have heard nothing from The Bishop of Winchester. . . . neither do I hear from The Weekly Post. . . . Aren't I corresponding with important people! The Bishop, Mr. Powys (and his wife) and The Editor of The Weekly Post (and his manager) . Lord!

> 5 November 35
>
> The Bishop and the Editor of The Diocesan Chronicle are both politely discouraging. My recent collection, The Place of Silence & other poems is in the hands of M/s Gollancz' reader, through the good offices of Frank Young[2]. . . . Last night Neptune Triumphant was produced at Pokesdown; thence to The Bell. . . . Drank beer and ate bread and cheese until 12:15. Still feel the effects slightly.

But Kenneth Hopkins did prepare himself for the visit— if the notes on the flap-side of the envelope from Miss Gregory are not later additions. In his hand are the titles *She Shall Have Music* and *King Log and Lady Lea*, two novels by Alyse Gregory; 1884, Llewelyn Powys' birth year; and the names of eighteen stories and novels by T. F. Powys—whom Hopkins tried to visit on the same trip to Chaldon, as sharp words in Llewelyn Powys' letters will tell. (In 1934, five Powys brothers and sisters lived within a one-mile trangle peaked north at Chaldon Herring: T. F. in the village itself, Gertrude, Philippa, and Llewelyn in the double farmhouse-cottage called Chydyok, and John Cowper at Rat's Barn, a farmhouse west of Chydyok. But by 1935 John had moved to North Wales.)

---

[1] In transcribing dates from the diary I have silently expanded (for example) 3/11/35 to 3 November 35.
[2] Then, as now, at Commin's, the Bournemouth bookshop.

There are four accounts of the first visit, no one of them by the ailing author. The day was a weekday, Wednesday, but Hopkins had been unemployed for several weeks. His firings are a recurrent theme in the Powys-Hopkins letters, but there are no details of this departure from Middleton & Co. Ltd. "I can't recall exactly why I got the sack from Holt's," he wrote in *The Corruption of a Poet*, "although I know my mother went round about it. In the same way, my leaving Middleton's is shrouded in mystery after all these years." The journal gives no clue, but in it, on the night of November 6, 1935, he wrote:

> This morning I left home at 9:00; stormy weather and a nasty wind. Arrived at Chaldon Herring 11:30, very wet, the rain having just ceased. Called at The Sailor's Return and proceeded to Mr. Llewelyn Powys' house. This is set quite alone, far up on the hill. I was very kindly received, and spoke to him for about 5 minutes.
>
> He enquired my means of livlihood, and commended the ironmongry trade. He spoke of poetry. "Live deeply," he said, "never be facetious or speak lightly of being a poet; ignore the success which is but a flash in the pan. Burn always with an intense flame, think always of beauty, never of the plaudits of men. Be proud of your calling as a member of the pilgrim band of poets." This is the gist of his words; possibly I have written it a little differently.
>
> He spoke of simplicity, and bade me write so. I have made a little poem from his words. Here it is:
>
> .   .   .   .   .
>
> I find on a second reading a measure of unworthiness in the poem, and therefore omit it.

Thirteen months later—after four visits to Chydyok, and two weeks after Llewelyn Powys' departure for Davos Platz—Hopkins gave more details:

> 13 December 36
>
> When I first met Llewelyn Powys he was over fifty years of age. He wore a white beard and a red dressing gown; he

was in bed. His room was small, with a sloping roof, and old, peeling, blue-distempered walls. Stained floor, simple furnishings. Books on shelves over his big bed, which occupied half the floor space. In one corner, a tiny stair-case to the upper floor.

At another time I saw him without his beard. He had the most beautiful smile* [Inserted with a darker pencil] * (absurd—like the man who had Lambs smile after he died) I have ever seen, slow and broad, and lasting. His speech was slow, his voice grave and low, the words delicately chosen to express exactly his thought, which they did to perfection. He made gestures with his hands as he spoke, slow gestures to match the slow heavy patterns, like tapestry, of his sentences.

He said to me, 'Great poetry does not fall from Heaven, it grows and has its roots in the earth.'

The fullest account of the first visit is in Hopkins' Introduction to *Llewelyn Powys: A Selection of his Writings* (London, 1952, and New York, 1961) :

It is seventeen years since, one wet November morning, I set out from Bournemouth on my bicycle to visit Llewelyn Powys. Of his work I then knew very little, and of himself nothing. It was enough for me, a lad of twenty, that he was a famous writer; for I hoped to become a famous writer too.
Accordingly, with a sheaf of my poems in my pocket and with my waterproof cape and leggings keeping out the worst of the weather, I pedalled through Poole, Lychett, Wareham, and across the rain-washed solitude of Thomas Hardy's Egdon Heath to the remote Dorset village of East Chaldon. . . .
And so, past a row of thatched grey cottages and up the slope I climbed until I reached the first smooth shoulder of the downs. Below me the small village of Chaldon—thatch and slate shining wet—appeared unpeopled under the racing clouds, except for the chimneys smoking. Before me lay nothing but slippery grass and a thin track worn into the chalk by centuries of rain and generations of wayfarers. This disappeared abruptly over the edge of the hill and re-

appeared across the valley on the side of an even steeper hill . . . at last, under the curious gaze of a group of cows, sheltering tail to wind in the lee of a sturdy barn, I came to Chydyok.

This farmhouse in which Llewelyn Powys lived stands almost at the summit of the second range of hills that divides East Chaldon from the coast. Just above Chydyok the cliffs fall five hundred feet sheer into the sea. . . .

The man I had come to visit was now fifty. To me he looked older, for his face was lined by illness and his eyes were deep set. He had a mass of curly, almost white hair, and a thick beard. The hand he held out to me was thin, with the blue veins clearly visible. His voice was not strong, but I thought its slow, rich tones the most remarkable I had ever heard. . . .

He lay propped against his pillows, yet, for all his illness, his eager interest in life was as strong as a young man's. I admired a red plaid shawl he was wearing, bright against the faded blue distemper of the wall. He told me the shawl had belonged to Edward Fitzgerald,[1] the translator of Omar Khayyam.

Alyse Gregory's second letter to Hopkins came in a package with the book of poems he had left at Chydyok, and her husband's letter giving his reactions to them.

AG–2: ALYSE GREGORY TO KENNETH HOPKINS

> Chydyok,
> Chaldon Herring,
> Dorchester, Dorset.
> November 7, 1935

Dear Mr. Hopkins,

I am returning your book with my husband's letter. I wish it might have as wide a reading as it deserves. We both admired the lively spirit in which you arranged its publication—and appreciated your gifts as a poet. I think it was wonderful of you to bicycle all these miles, and I felt

---

[1] The son of Fitzgerald's friend, William Bodham Donne, married Llewelyn's aunt, Catharine Johnson. The shawl came to Llewelyn from her.

concerned about your getting wet when I heard the rain come driving down.

With all best wishes for the sustaining of your muse's ardour, the independence of your mind, the daring of your imagination, and the subtlety of your insights, I am,

Sincerely yours,
Alyse Gregory

And in a letter of March, 1965, Miss Gregory wrote further of Kenneth Hopkins' visit at a time when "I fear he [my husband] was too ill":

> Visitors were for me a problem and an anxiety, but I do remember Mr. Hopkins as being most sensitive and tactful on that occasion.

Llewelyn Powys' response to Hopkins' nineteen poems is the keynote—in content and in tone—to the correspondence that continued for the next three and a half years. Dated the day of the visit, it was, of course, written in bed; "he used stiff-back exercise books," Miss Gregory wrote in May, 1965, "and wrote on his knee, propped up in bed."

LP–1: LLEWELYN POWYS TO KENNETH HOPKINS

Chydyok,
Chaldon Herring,
Dorchester, Dorset.
November 6, 1935

Dear Mr. Hopkins,

I have read your poems with interest—You certainly have what is most important of all intensity of feeling. I think I liked your love poems best especially the 2nd Sonnet, beginning[1]

—I think "the poet considers his soul" is the most original and I approved of your use of the rather daring word "bottom."

---

[1] He did not finish the paragraph.

—I think you are a poet and will always be a poet. I am afraid you will come to consider me as more of Moralist than a poet if I go on giving you instructions at the rate I have begun but I intend in this letter adding to what I have already said.

(1) To be a poet you must live with an intensity five times, nay a hundred times more furious than that of those about you. There is no scene, no experience which should not contribute to your poetic appreciations and culture.

(2) You must regulate your life as strict as a religious devotee— (A) you must keep a strict eye on your health— Live healthily—Though you go in rags be careful every day to wash every inch of your body—so it is always beautiful and *fresh*—even if you are too hard up to afford extravagant washing bills—wash your underclothes with your own hand —as though this extra personal fastidiousness were part of a religious rite. Never use powder or scent under any circumstance. In your eating keep as far as possible away from animal foods—eat dairy produce, fruit and vegetables. Always sleep with your windows wide open. Always try to take natural exercise. Aim at getting up half an hour earlier than other people and walking if possible to catch a glimpse of the sea *every morning*. These walks should be very important to gaining a heightened consciousness of your existence. The senses are most keen and receptive at such a time. Do the same if possible in the evening—sending your soul from your wrist like a Merlin hawk to fly to the stars—or to ride upon the winds or shiver in the rain above the housetops.

—Never try to assert yourself with your associates. Do not try to compete with them. Their way is not *your* way. Never use *their* weapons—be good natured and withdraw into your self. Always be simple and sensitive and direct—never facetious especially about poetry—Let them know nothing about it. Read, Read, Read, but never trivial books. Follow every person from whom you can learn anything. Keep a secret journal for the record of all the experiences of the day that seem to have value. Always look up in a dictionary the meaning of every word that you do not know and keep another little book for writing these words down. Rid your mind as far as you can of class consciousness, value intellect and sensibility and character—discount wealth as you discount poverty—avoid worldly ambition—let your ambition be elsewhere. Learn to discriminate, and to recognize what is vulgar and pretentious and trivial[,] be always simple and sincere and cast away all affectations. Be sensitively aware of everybody you have to do with.

As you grow more thoughtful and more poetic your personality will grow more arresting and you will find all the more attractive and exciting people will be drawn to you— Never pretend or show off and never waste a moment of your day.

With regard to your sexual life—Be able to be controlled and be able to be abandoned. Those who get most out of Love lie together on the enchanted web of Romance. Read the Oxford Book of English Verse over and over again. Study every line of John Keats and Matthew Arnold. Read a good translation of Lucretius, of Montaigne's Essays, of Rabelais, Read Andrew Lang's Iliad and Odyssey. Read all of Shakepeare's plays slowly, one a week. Bless you. Good luck.

Yours sincerely
Llewelyn Powys

[Around the margins of the first page]

Do your daily tasks carefully and conscientiously. It is important to be able to be economically independent—Do not be in any hurry to marry—Spend long hours in the libraries —join any literary societies—attend lectures, visit galleries— never miss any opportunity of learning about anything— Cultivate your love for the open Country—explore it[,] learn the names of every flower and bird. Linnets do not nest in woods—Your love of lonely places is a good sign— You can if you wish make your life a very thrilling one—you have many advantages—but you must look to yourself, examine your own soul and have little thought of cutting a figure—If you have an authentic passion for Life all else will be added.

The terse comment about linnets corrects their misplacement in a line by Hopkins: "... the woods where sing-

ing linnets nest." The "rather daring word 'bottom' " was
in this unpublished poem:

> The Poet considers his Own Soul
> from Every Angle
>
> I survey my soul from every side
> With steadilly diminishing pride:
> A piteous spectacle indeed!
>
> Again I contemplate the view
> From back, from bottom, from front, from top;
> But what has this to do with you?
>
> A third perusal I sustain:
> My stomach reels: I shall be ill!
> I dare not look at my soul again!

In his journal Kenneth Hopkins recorded his reactions
to the two letters from Chydyok. "My book of poems is
returned by Llewelyn Powys with a long letter the contents of which I have not yet fathomed," he wrote on
November 7, 1935. "I will copy it in here as soon as I
understand the whole of it; he is ill, and his writing fal-
ters." But Hopkins struggled manfully with the second
letter. "A note also from his wife, who writes very un-
intelligibly, but with much kindness. As far as I can make
out, she says: 'I am returning your book with my husband's
letter ....'" Eight long series of dots follow,
broken occasionally by words. Reading almost any Powys
letter is a battle slowly fought, but Hopkins won, as his
full answer, two days later, tells. While composing the
response he mused in his diary:

> I have not quite finished the reply to Mr. Powys, but shall
> post it tonight. He recommends me to keep a journal—like
> this, I suppose: but what information should it contain?—
> details of good eating, weather experienced, places visited,
> people seen—of thoughts and meditations, the inner life of
> the soul, and such matters?

I suppose a little of each. At all events, I arose at 10:15 this morning (Sunday) and ate ham for breakfast. I am contemplating a little plan to compose a poem out of my visit to him; perhaps to-day I will do some of it.

How do my methods compare with other poets, I wonder? I mean, as to the speed of composition, place, time of day, and such like. My longest poems are of about 120 lines —poems like The Wilderness, For Love that Dies, The Place of Silence. These are written straight down in about 2 hours with no pause till they are complete. After, except for minor corrections in punctuation, or of a single word, they are unaltered. Yet one reads of poets working for months, perhaps, at a single poem, not much longer than these. Why? Are they improving on the original draft, or do they compose only about ten lines a day? I think it is a great mistake to chop and change a poem once completed: one cannot (I cannot) recapture the original freshness and intensity of thought which we call inspiration.

KH–2: KENNETH HOPKINS TO LLEWELYN POWYS

125, Southcote Road
Bournemouth.
November 9, 1935

Dear Mr. Powys

It was a tremendous inspiration to me to see you personally and hear your advice; I shall never forget my first visit to you, but I hope in the spring, when you are in better health, to be allowed to see you again.

Every word of your letter betrays the keen interest you have taken in my visit and poems; I do not feel flattered at this, only humble that you should be so kind to a stranger, and proud that it is myself.

To me it seems wonderful that one so ill as you have been can write so long a letter; I cannot tell you how grateful I am.

Everything you have councelled me to do I shall to the best of my ability observe; the authors you recommend I

shall study carefully—Arnold I already know well, and
"Q" 's anthology.

I can see reason and wisdom in all your advice, save only
in this: the necessity to visit the sea *daily*—why daily I ask?
But I love the sea, and live almost in sight of it—I can walk
on the cliffs daily if I wish, and your instructions shall be
followed to the letter.

I did not wish you to return the book I left with you,
but no matter; when next I am in your village I will ask
you to accept another, containing a larger selection of my
poems.

When I left you on Wednesday I had lunch at the Inn,
and there learned that your brother, Mr. T. F. Powys was
living at Chaldon; I understood from your other brother's
Autobiography that he lived in Sussex; perhaps I mis-read
this. At all events, rather carried away by my enthusiasm
(for I have admired his books) I called at Mr. T. F. Powys
house, hoping to see him for a few minutes.

He was busy and could not talk to me. I tell you this because I fear he thought me very rude, and if you would convey to him my apologies I should feel more comfortable: impertinence was the last thing I intended, but I see now
that my action was ill-advised. Please tell him I am sorry.

I am not quite clear as to your meaning when you warn
me against competing with my associates, against asserting
myself, and the use of their weapons. But always I try to
emulate Landor's sentiment:

"I strove with none, for none was worth my strife"
I do not consciously regard myself as superior to others, but
I do disdain to quarrel with mankind.

In any case, I have many acquaintances, but few friends,
but these I love almost as myself.

In writing poetry, I agree wholly with Flecker: "The
Poet's function is to create beauty"—this first: all else is subordinate. I sometimes write light or satirical verse; this I
do chiefly as an exercise in manipulating words—I would
not publish any such verse—certainly none that I have so
far written.

A poet's job is not to teach: no. I, personally, am not equipped with any message or gospel for mankind; but if I can express a beautiful thought in beautiful words, I shall be content. Which is remembered now, the Ecclesiastical Sonnets of Wordsworth, or poems like "I wandered lonely as a cloud?"

I love lonliness for it's own sake, and melancholy; I love winter, and great winds, and the rain over the sea; of these I can more freely write than of sunshine and flowers. Similarly, I love to be with one or two chosen friends sitting in a little country inn; the crowds and life of the great cities bewilder me.

But I will not write more now; from time to time if I may, I will let you know how my work progresses and send you my latest verse; and any letter from you or Miss Gregory will be read and appreciated.

Please tell Miss Gregory that I shall long remember her kindness, and accept for yourself my good wishes and hope that you will continue recovering from your illness.

Yours sincerely
Kenneth Hopkins

AG–3: ALYSE GREGORY TO KENNETH HOPKINS

Chydyok,
Chaldon Herring,
Dorchester, Dorset.
November 11, 1935

Dear Mr Hopkins,

My husband wants me to thank you so much for your letter. He has not been so well these last few days and we try to keep him from the least exertion—so I am writing all his letters for him. He read your letter with pleasure, and we both hope we may see you, as you say, in the spring. Mr. T. F. Powys is very jealous of his solitude, and never sees any one if he can help it. You are fortunate in having friends (the fewer the safer) that you so love and trust.

With all best wishes,

Sincerely yours,
Alyse Gregory

References in Llewelyn Powys' second letter indicate a lost November letter from Hopkins, although his diary makes no mention of it.

LP-2: LLEWELYN POWYS TO KENNETH HOPKINS

> Chydyok,
> Chaldon Herring
> Dorchester, Dorset.
> [December 5, 1935]

Dear Mr Hopkins,

Thank you for your letter. I feel inclined to give you some advice as though you were my bastard and I Lord Chesterfield—You must not allow your feelings to be hurt—for there is no malice in me, only interest in your future. I will first try to indicate why I told you to go to the sea every day. We are all in danger of being trapped in our environments—a poet is saved from this by his appreciation of the mysteries of earth life—if you every day meditate even for a moment on the beauty and mystery of the sea—you bathe your mind in Eternity. The smell of it, the sound of it, the sight of it should enable you to forget the bath machines[1] and all modern vulgarities and realize that you are looking at what Homer looked at and all the long line of great poets,

"Sophocles long ago heard it on the Aegean"[2]

---

[1] Llewelyn Powys probably had not been on the public beach at Bournemouth for years—if ever. By 1935 these mobile bathhouses—large-wheeled, high-windowed, often horse-drawn dressing rooms some twelve feet high in which the Victorian bather changed clothes while being transported across the beach and into deeper water—were obsolete.

[2] In *Skin for Skin,* telling of his father's first visit after the initial attack of tuberculosis, Llewelyn wrote:

My father came to see me and prayed at my bedside, his head white as . . . a dove's wing against a thunder-cloud. . . . Presently, when my father had finished his supplication and was no longer kneeling on the bare rain-washed boards which, from his Victorian point of view, were so unspeakably depressing, I persuaded him to read me certain poems of Matthew Arnold. "He was not so good a man as his father," he said emphatically.

It should become to you a symbol of release and an elixir for the imagination and you should never pass it by with philistine apathy.

—You have much to learn. I have seldom received a more foolishly facetious letter than your first to me—You must understand that even amongst free spirits and poets manners are to be valued highly and the test of good manners is to be more concerned about another person's attitude than your own. When I saw you I was won by a certain personal charm that you have and this prompted me to write you so careful a letter—but now comes this letter which is discouraging because it takes too much for granted—You must prove yourself sensitive and understanding before you expect to be taken in by anyone—

It was indiscreet of you to call on my brother without having given him any warning. You certainly have no reason to say that you will continue to call me Mr Powys,[3] as though by way of concession—and you should not expect to take as your right advantages which come to people who are full of reserve and diffidence and sensitive understandings. I advise you to look about amongst your friends and model your behaviour after the demeanour of the one that is most sensitive—I would look in all directions, for gentlemen have no monopoly of good conduct and often the messenger boy is more sensitive to another's personality than a Prince. You must avoid being cheap and self assertive—You have undoubted gifts but do not talk nonsense about "inspiration." You must learn to go over and over your poetry. You must improve your mind in every way, *not for show*. You should approach English Literature like a scholar with real application.

Say always less than you know and be more eager to listen than to speak. At present you are not above magazine level but you could, I believe, develope—It depends on your

[3] Throughout their acquaintance, Kenneth Hopkins never used any form of address but "Mr. Powys." A year and a half later, after corresponding with Louis Wilkinson for some months, he sought and received permission to call him "Louis"; and after a bantering exchange of letters in the spring of 1938, Hopkins was encouraged to call John Cowper Powys "Uncle John."

spiritual intensity which should be inexhaustable—I am very happy you have so delightful a relationship—She may be able to teach you many things. Examine yourself always very closely as in your poems—and avoid vanity and conceit but build your life up on a solid foundation until you are superior to all your handicaps but build on the *inside* where none sees—Be determined now that you are still young to become a really deeply cultured man and a poet— and never lose sight of your intention no not for an hour. I send you my blessing.

Yours sincerely
Llewelyn Powys

[Across the top of page one]

I liked your poem very much. It is the best I have seen of yours and *is* far above magazine level. Send it to The New English Weekly, 38 Cursitor Street London.

On a transcript of this second letter, in my possession, are marginal comments by Kenneth Hopkins. The *she* of "She may be able to teach you many things" is starred, and the name "Margaret" is in red in the margin; later, in black ink, he wrote, "or perhaps Muriel." A recent poem by Hopkins (*and* John Cowper Powys), published in *Philobiblon*, Number Seven (Hamilton, New York, 1965), illuminates but does not clarify these notes. As the fourth stanza tells, the first stanza with its parenthetic "something's" was written by John Cowper Powys in a letter to Hopkins (on December 6, 1937):

A BALLAD OF MAIDENS THREE

The sands are (something), the winds are wet,
And over the (something) my sail is set
With Muriel, Doris and Margaret.

The clouds are drifting, the pimpernel
Blooms bright in the lanes I love so well
With Margaret, Doris and Muriel.

The moon is shining and sweet it is
Under the silvery moon to kiss
With Margaret, Muriel, and Do-ris!

This ballad is copyright. J. C. P.
Composed in a letter lines one, two, three,
And the nine that are left have been written by me.
                                        Kenneth Hopkins

Hopkins has described his first meeting with T. F. Powys
as appreciably shorter than his minutes with Llewelyn.
When Theodore answered the knock at his door in Chaldon Herring, Hopkins started to explain that he had just
come from Llewelyn's; but, before he had fully introduced
himself, Theodore mumbled a few words and turned inside. The incident stayed long in Llewelyn's mind as the
antithesis of Chesterfield's way. In two letters a year later
(LP–19 and LP–22) he referred to the precipitate call
on T. F., and counseled further reading of Lord Chesterfield's *Letters to his Son*.

Hopkins' answer to this second letter is also missing—
as are some two-thirds of his letters to Llewelyn Powys—
but his journal for the period records a variety of activities
and moods, with poetry, as always, central in his thoughts.
He described the making of a sonnet, one rainy afternoon
on the cliffs above Bournemouth, and the caressing of a
girl three nights later—interrupting to say that "if my
diary is published at any time, it will have to be expurgated
like the Arabian Nights." His concern was unwarranted,
even from the standpoint of a bath-machine moralist. He
was lonely as he approached his twenty-first birthday—"no
money, few friends"—and quarreled with his family about
his birthday gift: some days later it arrived, a large bookcase bought from Norman Colbeck—in 1935, as in 1967, an
amiable bookseller in Bournemouth. And Hopkins commenced *Up Till Now, Chapters of Autobiography* in the
journal, portions of which continue to appear for several
months. But the first installment—two chapters that take

him into his school years—is interrupted by a more current event:

> I landed a job with Hooper and Ashby's
> to begin on December 2.

LP-3: LLEWELYN POWYS TO KENNETH HOPKINS

Chydyok,
Chaldon Herring,
Dorchester, Dorset.
[n.d.][1]

Dear Mr. Hopkins,

It was very kind of you to send me the poem.[2] I think you
have done well. Indeed I enjoyed reading it very much indeed and am very glad to have it—I would not explain it
but let the poem explain itself—the word "sexual" is a difficult word to bring near poetry and "lechery" not much
better. Your treatment is full of charm and sensitiveness
and I liked well the last lines indicating how unutterable
was the gift of Aphrodite.

—I am very pleased that you have acquired that good
edition[3] of Rabelais—Sir Thomas Urquart is wonderful
with this translation, he died of laughter at hearing of the
return of Charles II to England. I advise you to read with
concentration and not skim—choosing only the more outrageous passages as I used to do as a young man. I would
do the same with Andrew Lang's translation of the Iliad

---

[1] The original envelope is missing. Hopkins' listing, on December
29, of books recently acquired includes Llewelyn Powys' *Cup-Bearers
of Wine and Hellebore;* the substitute envelope bears the note, in
Hopkins' hand, "This contained an inscribed copy of *Cup-Bearers.*"
The diary also tells that two letters were received from Powys in
December. This letter surely came between December 6 and December 29, 1935.

[2] Diary passages suggest that the poem might have been "This
Transient Dream," or "The Rape of Sylvia Trust." Neither is now
available.

[3] The Moray Press edition (Derby, n.d.) with Doré illustrations.
Llewelyn misspells *Urquhart,* but I find no justification for correct-
ing his two or three errors while allowing Hopkins' to stand.

and Odyssey—You cannot give too much attention to these books. They will have a lasting influence on your work and lift it out of any provincial limitations. I would also read Christopher Marlowe very carefully especially Faustus and Hero and Leander—He will be a great inspiration to you— As John Keats used to do make a point of looking up the various classical deities mentioned—until you are very familiar with these old stories. I would also read Don Quixote very slowly and carefully and I should keep a note book near you to copy out anything that especially hits your fancy.[4] If you read slowly and with *intelligence*—Homer, Lucretius, Shakespeare, Cervantes, Montaigne, Rabelais you will have won more health to your spirit than you would have got from three years at the University.[5] I would be very eclectic in your reading—I would try to outgrow your taste for writers who are not quite first rate—amongst them I would certainly class Belloc and Chesterton and Flecker and Rupert Brooke—They are good but not good enough. As a boy I used to read a great deal of Stevenson and he helped my style but I remember my brother John deploring my taste and he also is not quite *sound*—Consider for instance his likening the earth "to a lukewarm bullet" [in "An Apology for Idlers"] and then read Milton's Hymn to the Nativity with the conception of the world being on hinges! Second rate minds are inclined to liken "great

---

[4] John Cowper Powys, in commenting on Llewelyn's allusive style and his love for "our best and most memorable old writers" (in the introduction to the combined edition of *Somerset and Dorset Essays*—London, 1957) wrote: "Thus the whole literature of our island has become an immemorial palimpsest, richer, sweeter, more suggestive, more significant than it could possibly have been if each individual writer had prided himself on showing off his own confounded caprices rather than on being naturally and instinctively himself."

[5] Hopkins has recently said that when, in their first meeting, he deplored his lack of education, Llewelyn Powys pointed out that ironmongery was earthy, elemental, and important—in contrast to many occupations—and that the best writers were down-to-earth, and not always university-bred. About the "stupid sentence" reference in this paragraph Hopkins says: Mr. Powys was perhaps right, but I had only three choices—to ignore his remark, to argue with it, or to apologize. Now, as then, I would elect the third.

things" to "little things"—they want to treat them on *fam-
liar ground*. Even now I did not find your letter satisfactory
—"I am very sorry that parts of my last letter *offended or
hurt you*"—that was a stupid sentence. Before you write or
speak to another human being you must leap like a grasshopper clear out of your skin and with an imaginative effort put yourself in his place. In this letter you still presup-
pose too much—do not really appreciate the blunder in
manners that you made but rather deftly "pass the bean"
back to me—and you are really not in a position to do this—
for so far you have not proved yourself—I have only seen
you for a few moments and you write as if you were already
on equal terms with me and that I was as vulnerable to
your words as any familiar companion of yours—"Have not
I in my time heard lion's roar?"[6]—I can only give you hints
in these matters—You must puzzle them out. In your rela-
tions with girls it is essential to get out of your own skin and
watch their delicate evasive psyches wavering to and fro as
a cat watches a mouse[7]—and keep casting the golden net of
your imagination about them and they will grant you the
most charming favours. Even in ordinary life—you should
study to make yourself charming to everybody you come in
contact with—saying and doing just the things that prove
you are *aware* of their peculiar tastes and characteristics—
this is what separates the philistine world from the world of

---

[6] The phrase was used often by Llewelyn after his return from
Africa, both in a caterwauling sense, and broader reference to the
heady outside world. In March, 1920, he wrote to John in America
(numbers 86 and 88 in the *Letters*):
   The idea of returning to school mastering in England is more
   than distasteful. "Have I not in my time heard lions roar?" . . .
   How terrible this growing old is. Here I am nearly 36 and nothing done, my writing found out, come to nothing, and no secure
   work found yet. I feel a shirker and dilletante[sic]. In my dis-
   tress I hold out hands to you. . . . [later] Surely my feeling of
   futility is the result of being in this backwater [Dorset] where I
   have no scope or is it that I really am one of these University
   men unfitted for anything and incapable of carrying through any
   enterprise—but then I was a successful sheep farmer.
[7] In the Introduction to her husband's *Letters* Alyse Gregory wrote:
"I remember his once saying to me that all writing was 'but a
whistling to make mice dance.'"

civil spirits and you should practice it till it becomes a second nature to you on everybody but always suppressing your own Ego so that *it is not visible*—though below the surface it steadily grows deeper and wiser—gathering experience from any chance spirit and encounter.

Yours sincerely
Llewelyn Powys

[Vertically, in the top margin of page one]

I do not like your using the word "ivorine." This should be altered—It is sentimental and hybrid—Ivory is such a beautiful and poetical word—This suggests the invention of a Haberdasher's publicity agent!

LP-4: LLEWELYN POWYS TO KENNETH HOPKINS

Chydyok,
Chaldon Herring,
Dorchester, Dorset.
February 18, 1936

Dear Mr Hopkins
Thank you for your letter. I would be glad to see you on Sunday morning as near to 11:30 as is convenient for you. The chain was originally placed under Bats Head for the convenience of the coastguards. The Bottom above is known locally as Chainy Bottom—and retains many traces of a Bronze Age settlement. I will talk of your poem when I see you.

Yours sincerely
Llewelyn Powys

LP-5: LLEWELYN POWYS TO KENNETH HOPKINS

Chydyok
[February 27, 1936]

Dear Mr Kenneth Hopkins,
We hope you got back safely and were none the worse for your exertion. I have read the book of poems you were so good as to copy out for me. A Pinewood Memory with its

Dedication ["to Muriel"] has some charming lines but it is too much of an unreal sexual fantasy for my complete literary acquiescence. I would experiment a little outside the romantic. I would try writing from your actual experience converting into poetry the very dust of every day life as poets alone can do—Turning all into gold—

I mean try to get into poetry the actual smack of your amorous encounters—How the girl or boy affects your senses, the boards of the room the tile of the floor—the brooch she wears, the smell of her body—the banalities she utters which are unable to kill your admiration—the stars shining down as the garden gate clicks at her departure—the misery of having to be parted from her, your savage hatred of the shop with its smell of oil and polish and nails—the liberation that a glimpse of the sea gives you. Try to leave Fantasy and get down to the reality of pots and pans [;] out of such inauspicious matter poetry will leap new born.

Experiment! Try to catch actuality off its guard with the sunlight of *eternity* glancing upon it as it does upon the floor of your shop when some unpleasant customer stands there gaping, thereby in a trice reducing all human values to nothing—Your girl will be beautiful and magical enough to leap out of the ashes like a Phoenix bird. Have no fear. Her thighs, her ankles remain classical and Helen Quondam was not more alluring. I like very much the two lines

> Do you think I love you less,
> Comrade once of happiness

Also the poem which begins

> Love you thought a jest or toy

and also

Song

> If I softly, shyly kiss

What you really want to do in your poetry is to redeem stark reality—Anyhow try—Try new experiments and do not waste an hour—live with "a gem like flame." I was very pleased by the intelligent interest you showed in all that you see like the little picture of Rabelais' house and Akhenaton—I am sending this star book[1]—I thought it might interest your friend. Dont waste an hour—

Bless you

Yours sincerely
Llewelyn Powys

Although details of this second visit to Llewelyn Powys, on Sunday, February 23, 1936, were not entered in Hopkins' ledger-journal, it was probably at this time that Powys gave him an ancient Egyptian scarab. In a transcript of this letter, opposite the phrase "your savage hatred of the shop," Hopkins has written, "But I never hated it. I am still fascinated by the smell of timber, tar, and linseed oil." But odors, prime vehicles of nostalgia, may mellow: in his journal entry for March 7, 1936, in the Second Preface (of four facetious prefaces) to a proposed volume of essays, *Thus Have I Thought,* Hopkins wrote:

> I work all the week at a Builders Merchant's, loading lorries and unloading lorries, and smelling their awful stench. Do you like the smell of lorries, starting cold in the morning? Few viler things are known to me; very few, and those not to be spoken of here. I see all the week merry sights like piles of bricks and heaps of empty lime bags and baths and corrugated iron. I hear the most diverting things, like the foreman's rendering of Sankey's hymns, or the manager speaking over the telephone to a man who owes money to the firm, and seeks further credit. I taste cement, creosote, rust, sawdust. I tread among dusty shelves. Don't you think it's clever of me to write a book in which no mention is made of these disgusting things? I assure you, nothing herein treats of the ironmongery trade; Lord, no!

The first essay for *Thus Have I Thought* tells of a play produced for the Vicar's garden party:

---

[1] *The Monthly Evening Sky Map* (Brooklyn: Leon Barritt). The envelope from Brooklyn, postmarked 1936, was used by Powys to send the booklet and his letter. Hopkins passed the map on to Paul French, his best friend, now a chiropodist in Bournemouth.

The chief difficulty was to find a play suitable for the open air; finally, in despair, I wrote one myself, adapting it from my epic poem The Defense of Suggsbodyville.

The play was called Utterpug the Terrible: a tragedy of elemental passions, and a bare three weeks before the show I called my first rehearsal. The cast was as good as any we might hope to collect, consisting of our very best actors. Steve, who weighs eighteen stone, threw herself into the part of Felicia the Winsome. Alan, all five foot of him, was the hero, Otherwiggle the Craven. We had Procky for the villain, Turgid the Bold, and for Utterbug the Terrible good fortune secured us, Frankland Rigby himself.

But, as *The Corruption of a Poet* tells—before giving a three-page sampling from the dialogue of *Utterpug the Terrible*—"the non-arrival of Miss Stevens, detained on business in Nottingham, left the producer H. K. Hopkins no alternative but to play the heroine himself."

Powys' "gem like flame" quotation is one of some forty passages and phrases omitted from the 1949 Bodley Head edition of the letters to Kenneth Hopkins. Alyse Gregory, who, with the assistance of Louis Wilkinson, edited that volume, had written earlier of certain tendencies in her husband's prose, "more particularly in his early writing, to reflect his close reading of such writers as Charles Lamb and Walter Pater, something approaching the precious not wholly indigenous to his own strong native gifts."

These are the poems that Llewelyn Powys liked; all three appeared in early collections, and the second is in Hopkins' *Collected Poems: 1935–1965*:

Song

Do you think I love you less
Comrade once of happiness
Now for ever lost to me,
Dearly loved and lost to me?

All our friendship fled away
Like the mist that holds brief sway

At the dawning on the hills
Mist of morning on the hills.

All I ever loved in you,
Laughter, youth, the love we knew
Briefly, gladly, long ago:
I have lost them long ago.

The Jest

Love you thought a jest or toy
For your least diversion fashioned;

I was an amusing boy
Teasing you with lips impassioned;

This was nothing true or real,
This was frolic, lightly spoken;

You are deaf to my appeal,
And by you my heart is broken.

Song

If I softly, shyly kiss,
Lightly, only thy sweet breast
Is there wrong or shame in this?

Dearest heart, accept my kiss,
Tis my love made manifest;
I have lived, would die, for this.

Early in March, 1936, A. R. Powys died, "betrayed by his animal pride in his body," Llewelyn wrote to Rivers Pollock, "the pride of a horse going up a hill—till his heart stops." "Brother Positive," as the family called the fourth brother, was in his fifty-fifth year, and the first of the ten adult Powyses to die. Llewelyn's own health was rarely mentioned in his letters to Hopkins, but in a letter to Van Wyck Brooks written during A. R.'s illness he said:

I truly believe I am getting better. What a chance if after being in bed for three years I return to life as merry as ever and even the grasshopper no longer a burden. Ho! Ho! . . .

We have been reading Chaucer with such deep appreciation. I truly think he is the greatest English poet after Shakespeare, greater than Spenser or Milton. Oh! how mellow and frank and free, and no moralic acid and no catechism.

LP-6: LLEWELYN POWYS TO KENNETH HOPKINS

[Chydyok
March 6, 1936]

Dear Mr Kenneth Hopkins,

I was very happy to know you enjoyed yourself after your visit and the next week-end as well. We thought it so kind of you to have occupied yourself with our affairs and I am very glad to know where I can get these note books. I liked them because their backs looked as if they were made out of pressed green rushes—I envied you those night walks—It is true you cannot be happier than when you are near to nature, even suffering her hardships. I think perhaps I will wait to see your plays—I have very little sense of the comic and am not too good at reading plays. Your poetry always interests me.

I like to think of the eager intellectual life of you, and your friends. Remy de Gourmont said "To live is to grow wise and sceptical."

Yours sincerely
Llewelyn Powys

KH-3: KENNETH HOPKINS TO LLEWELYN POWYS

125, Southcote Road
Bournemouth.
April 11, 1936

Dear Mr. Powys,

You will have heard of the mishap at White Nose on Good Friday, and you may know that my friends and I were concerned in it. A very inaccurate account is to be read in the local papers, but I expect you will be interested to know the truth, which is this:

We had caught the early train which leaves Bournemouth at 2:20 (a.m.) and reached the cliff top at Middle Bottom about dawn, if anything, rather later. We descended by the Smuggler's Path (partly by the aid of a rope, and not without difficulty) and explored as far as possible to the east. We then made tea on a primus stove, and breakfasted.

After some time we made our way towards White Nose, and with very little trouble came within about 50 yards of the end, where (I take it) is the cave you mention in your writings. About at this point the rocks are much larger and suddenly I saw my friend disappear down a crevase. I was about 10 yards behind and our companion as far again behind me. I found my friend being buffeted in and out of the little crack by the sea, and by jumping down on to a ledge I easilly caught him by the belt and secured him upon the rock beside me. The third of our party now appeared. Between us we got the victim to a dry spot and wrapped him in what little dry clothing we had—for the water had been breaking over us all, but two coats lay safely upon the beach where we had left them.

I then returned up the cliff by way of our rope, to Chaldon and telephoned the boat-owners at Lulworth. When I rejoined my companions the injured one was conscious and walking to meet the boat. He was taken to Lulworth and I, and the other walked by way of the path, reaching Lulworth about one o'clock.

We hired a car to take us to Wool and arrived home about 4 o'clock. The affair might have been very serious, owing to the danger of drowning; as it was, all ended happily and we are none the worse.

The Fountain Rock looks magnificent from below; I had no camera, but I shall return and photograph it.

A few weeks ago we penetrated almost right round White Nose from the west, but the tide defeated us for the last few yards.

I was at Wookey Hole[1] last week, and of course I thought of "A Glastonbury Romance" as the guide recited his little

---

[1] Llewelyn Powys' "Wookey Hole" in *Somerset Essays* tells of a visit with his brother John to this ancient cavern in the Mendips which served as a setting for John's *A Glastonbury Romance*. This

lecture. One day I hope I may meet your brothers. (I mean those who write books) I do want very much to make the acquaintance of Mr. J. C. Powys; do you think it will be possible on one of my visits to you?

I hope I may come to Chydyok soon, will you let me know when I may?

I have read "The Beardsley Period,"[2] but I wish to look into it again if I am not keeping it too long? I fancy the author knows his subject very well; I like his style, too.

There is a book I bought recently which I know will interest you, but you may have read it. It is:
"Letters of Lady Hesketh to the Rev. John Johnson Lld. concerning their kinsman, William Cowper the Poet, edited by Catharine Bodham Johnson (nee Donne)[3] with portraits, published in 1901 by Jawold and Sons.

This book is in excellent condition, and cost me 4d, which shows that bargains may still be had by those who seek. I will send or bring it if you have not a copy.

At the present time my poetry is rather at a standstill. I wrote one fairly long poem, but I hesitate to send it, it seems so poor. Of course, my first ventures in a new method must be so; but as I write the manuscript is mis-laid, so I will find it, and revise it, and send it next time. However, I enclose one or two earlier pieces.

Please remember me to Miss Gregory.

I will now say good-bye.

Yours sincerely
Kenneth Hopkins

The accident occasioned a second, almost equally brief meeting between Kenneth Hopkins and T. F. Powys. Re-

---

novel, and fourteen other books by John Cowper Powys, are being reissued—or issued for the first time in America—by Colgate University Press, Hamilton, New York, in collaboration with Macdonald & Co., London.

[2] Osbert Burdett, *The Beardsley Period* (London, 1935).

[3] The daughter of Fitzgerald's friend, William Bodham Donne. Her grandmother was the sister of "Johnny of Norfolk."

membering, perhaps, the earlier rebuke about the indiscretion of his November call, Kenneth did not tell Llewelyn that as he ran back from the cliff, he came first to Theodore's house, clambered over a fence (ignoring a gate some yards away), burst in through the orchard, and shouted for a phone. T. F. came slowly to a window with a book in his hand, deliberated the problem, then politely suggested that he thought, perhaps, that the post office might have a phone—he was not sure.

And Hopkins' account of the accident under the White Nose was certain to provoke for Llewelyn Powys memories of the real tragedy there, two years after he moved into the coastguard cottage—a story told with simple sorrow in "A Grave in Dorset" published in *Earth Memories* in 1934. Walter Franzen, an American friend, was killed, and Powys had written of the Rock that Hopkins proposed to photograph:

> He fell a little to the east of the Fountain Rock. What a monument Fate has prepared for him! Here indeed was a cenotaph, we thought, as we stood by the side of that mighty bastion ribbed with flint. If his neck had to be broken, this place was well selected.

LP-7: LLEWELYN POWYS TO KENNETH HOPKINS

Chydyok
Chaldon Herring
Dorchester
April 14, 1936

Dear Mr Hopkins,

I am very glad the adventure at White Nose turned out no worse—I thought you behaved with great spirit and resolution and I think you undoubtedly saved Mr Roberts' life by your good sense and I felt proud of you. I know how extremely agitating such mischances can be to a sensitive mind. I will get you to tell me the whole story when you next visit me—I would suggest a date towards the end of May as the most suitable as then I hope to be very much better.

My eldest brother, Mr John Cowper Powys is living in North Wales. I try always to keep people away from him as he is so full of concern for everybody's feelings that he is liable to be exploited by numbers of unrewarding people but I will bear your request in my mind and if a suitable occasion arises for introducing you will do so. I very much appreciated the enterprize you and your friends showed in coming so early onto these downs. I think you will satisfy your desire to become a notable poet if you keep on building from the bottom and never waste so much as a half hour of your life and separate yourself from everything that is insincere and loud and hollow—I am again having trouble with my eyes[1] but in a day or two I will write to you about your poems.

I am glad you came to no mischance under White Nose.

Yours sincerely
Llewelyn Powys

AG-4: ALYSE GREGORY TO KENNETH HOPKINS

Chydyok,
Chaldon Herring,
Dorchester, Dorset.
April [14, 1936]

Dear Mr. Hopkins,

I am sorry not to have answered your letter before, but truly the combination of my errant mind and the demands that are made upon it alien to my indolent intellectual tastes make it difficult for me to get to my writing table where I find letters accumulating at an alarming rate. My husband is better, but visits are always a great anxiety—and I find myself often appearing to assume a similar rôle to that of

---

[1] A recurrent problem starting shortly after the severe hemorrhages that left him an invalid. In June, 1934, in the continuation of a correspondence initiated by Eleanor Roosevelt, Franklin Roosevelt wrote: "I am sorry indeed to learn about the overstraining of your eyes and I trust that you are giving them full opportunity to 'come back' and let you start on your excellent work again. . . . I have, as you can well understand, a horror of being accused of preaching. I think I can be of most service by [*sic*] the development of liberal ideas by taking one hurdle at a time. . . ."

Gorki's mistress who stands between him and anxious callers as inexorably as a bolted door. My husband seems stronger than he is and this misleads even his dearest friends into indiscretions for which they would otherwise be on the look out.

You have been most considerate and thoughtful and I hope in a few weeks more time we shall be able to set a day for you to call—for it is a pleasure to my husband to see you and talk to you—and I have such sympathy for the quick blood and whirling impetuous certain thoughts of youth— and for all that is free moving and erratic—that I value subtlety, restraint, irony, and sophisticated manners almost as much—But I am impatient and am just trying to begin to begin to write an essay—though this is of little importance— for the written word I think has gathered to itself an undue veneration. The mind should be a gimlet to search out true ore—and not to anxiously demand attention—and many a man has been struck down in his full manhood by the desire for success or even fame and never risen again.

Sincerely yours,
Alyse Gregory

KH-4: KENNETH HOPKINS TO ALYSE GREGORY

125, Southcote Road
Bournemouth.
April 30, 1936

Dear Miss Gregory,

Thank you for your letter, with the good news it contains. I was very anxious when I heard of the increase in Mr. Powys' illness. I am writing a brief note to him also.

I appreciate your difficulty with correspondence. I have few letters to write, but always I have books accumulating which I must read, and I never catch up with the pile. There seems in life too little time, even for doing what one wishes to do—and yet there are things to be done which are against one's wishes!

Bournemouth is looking very beautiful now, with the gardens newly arrayed, and many fine new buildings. I think Mr. Powys does not greatly like the town, but really there are few to surpass it. I prefer the country, but if I must live in town I think this is as lovely as any. I wonder if you have ever been here? In St. Peter's Churchyard daffodils grow wild, and close by upon Horseshoe Common the children fish for newts: I fished myself in years gone by, with as much success. A year or two ago a fox was seen in the common—within a stone's throw of the centre of the town.

Two sparrows are busy nesting just outside the premises where I work. I put straw out on the pavement, and they seem grateful, fluttering down and selecting the largest and cleanest whisps, some fifteen inches long. The nest is just under a gable, and is reached—when the load is heavy—in three short flights—up to the wall, pause, on to the top of the rainwater pipe, pause, and on again to the next, where a great hauling in of the burden!

I am afraid I neglect my work to watch them. Occasionally another little bird comes for straw, but he flies beyond the building, and I have not traced his nest.

Yours sincerely
Kenneth Hopkins

LP-8: LLEWELYN POWYS TO KENNETH HOPKINS

[Postcard:
May 4, 1936]

Thank you for your letter. I will write to you about your poems in a day or two—I am very glad you have managed to get a good edition of Don Quixote—I beg you to give the book your most serious attention—I will find a day for your next visit before so very long—This cold wind is very tiresome.

Yours sincerely
Llewelyn Powys

LP-9: LLEWELYN POWYS TO KENNETH HOPKINS

Chydyok,
Chaldon Herring,
Dorchester, Dorset.
May 25, 1936

Dear Mr Kenneth Hopkins

At last I am returning your early poems. The delay is due to my having lent them to Miss Sylvia Townsend Warner and Miss Valentine Ackland,[1] which was perhaps foolish as they did not rouse in them any real interest. Of course the poems are as you know immature—I did not care for some of them, especially those with a humorous turn. I thought the amorous passages far the best—but very much deplored a certain hesitation or spiritual irresolution in these as if the Christian teaching was working like some injected virus and prevented your mind moving naturally and freely. Your diatribe against seducers for example which in the end turned into guilty self accusations marred a poem[2] that should have been scandalous and happy—That seduced girls do sometimes become harlots is the result of economic conditions—Women who too often sacrifice their deeper emotional life to the momentary gratification of the senses are inclined to become hard, but so are self interested old maids.

Often, however, a girl's life is enriched by an early sexual initiation, especially if they possess natures simple and clear and untimidated by the ethos of the Avenue! I think in

---

[1] Sylvia Townsend Warner and Valentine Ackland, then living near Chaldon, were good friends of the Powyses before and after the law case involving conditions in the girls' home. (Some of Llewelyn's harshest words of literary criticism—directed against Ernest Hemingway—appear in his *Letters,* addressed to Miss Ackland.) Miss Warner's *Lolly Willowes,* first of her many novels, was the Book-of-the-Month Club's initial selection, in 1926; their joint collection of poems, *Whether a Dove or a Seagull* (1933) , was issued without signatures on the individual poems; in 1936, Miss Ackland wrote *Country Conditions,* a study of the village laborer in contemporary England.

Kenneth Hopkins gave money to Miss Warner's subscription for Loyalist Spain in 1937, and a sonnet, "Because your heart so mourns for stricken Spain," the proceeds from which were to go to the fund, if she could sell it. She answered that a decent modesty should alter the title ("To Sylvia Townsend Warner") , and that it was not easy "to persuade editors to pay for poetry. They seem to look on it as a sort of dandelion, that can be had for the picking." The poem was not sold. In 1944, poems by Sylvia Townsend Warner were published in Private K. Hopkins' Grasshopper Broadsheets.

[2] The MSS of the six-page poem, "Men Call It Love," and its recasting in 1937 as "The Progress of Love" are in the Hopkins Collection at the University of Texas.

England more marriages are broken up or become unhappy through sexual frigidity than through an excess of eroticism which is always exciting and often spreads a sense of natural happiness far and wide. This poem was spoilt by your faltering—You should have had the courage of your pen.

It might have been written by Byron at Le Havre—but the one line that ends with "finding the place all right" did jar a little—You should have turned your moral indignation against the *insensitiveness* of professional seducers—their crudeness, and greed, and lack of understanding. It should be a matter of pride with you that no girl with whom you have been happy should ever feel regrets about it—and even the most glancing encounter should ensure for them your life-long gratitude and appreciation *and* love. How ever badly they may behave afterwards *the grace they have once shown you* absolves them from everything. Do you remember how one of Goethe's girls was asked why she had never married and answered "The heart that Goethe loved could never love another"—and love affairs should always be rich and full and happy and free from misgivings and recriminations which so disfigure the affairs of the ungenerous.

Yours sincerely
Llewelyn Powys

PS.

Would you be able to discover for me how much the Bournemouth Pigeon Fancier would sell me a pair of breeding fan tail pigeons, of no particular pedigree—and also whether there is a shop where I could buy water snails and a pair of large gold fish or other ornamental fish to suit the close quarters of our pond? Also I received from some Bournemouth second hand book shop which you may know (I fancy it is the most important one) [3] a notice of their stock and in this booklet was listed a volume of the coats of arms of the Landed Gentry of England (coloured) —The book was published at £2..10..0 and they are selling it at 15/—I cant remember the bookseller's name but if you located such a book—I would be interested although I daresay this odd mediaeval interest of mine will never persuade

[3] Horace G. Commin was, I believe, the only Bournemouth bookseller then issuing catalogues regularly.

me when it comes to the point of disbursing so many honest shillings on so pretty "a work of fiction"—Perhaps the bookseller would be willing for me to see it on approval—The book was first published five or six years ago—but the bookseller's name I do not know, nor the author's name.

[Written vertically in the margins of page one]

With regard to your coming to see me. Unfortunately I am not as sound as I hoped to be—but if you send me a card of warning I will see you for a *strict twenty minutes.* I have been not so well the last few days and my temperature is still a little uncertain and there are many people that I *must* see, so that if I am to get through this summer without relapse it is absolutely essential for me to be careful.

Llewelyn Powys' disregard of conventional morality was frequently and clearly stated—"All ethical imperatives are man-made"; "trust to your senses"; "the only purpose of life is to live"—but only Alyse Gregory, in her Introduction to his *Letters,* spoke openly of how he practiced them. Whether or not a reader champions the "ethos of the Avenue," he must credit Powys with consistency of belief and action. Miss Gregory wrote:

My brother-in-law John thought my husband's one "serious" fault was "trying to make secret love to his friends' girls," which seems more like a *folie* than a fault.

> Friendship is constant in all other things,
> Save in the office and affairs of love.

Llewelyn himself always said to me that his fault was treachery, but I never discovered anything that could be really given this name except in the matter referred to by my brother-in-law; and I would as soon think of expostulating against such treacheries as against the winds of heaven. For where does treachery begin and where does it leave off? Who does not perceive evil in what goes against him and virtue in his own desires? . . . Llewelyn was a lover of life and ever susceptible to the graces of that amiable sex one of

Dear Mr.Powys,

I am typing this letter because I would spare you
the agony of deciphering my handwriting,and because I
feel there is a better chance of beguiling you into
reading right to the end.

I suppose I am impertiment to address you at all;
at all events,that is nothing to the impertinence I now
contemplate,which is no less a thing than inviting myself to call upon you at your home one morning.
However,I have some trace of good maners,even if,in my
haste,I do omit the second "n";therefore it is that I
warn you of my intention,so that,if the thought of a
stranger in your house really appals you beyond bearing
you can write and reject my proffered friendship with
strange and terrible oaths-and be very sure I shan't
blame you.

I am a precocious young man of twenty-one,with a
higher opinion of my own value as a poet than any man
in England,and a vast determination to Make my Mark in
Life-and also a vast disinclination to exert myself in
furthering this end.

For yourself and your writings I have a great respect,
which I mention now because if and when I see you I shall
undoubtedly talk of nothing but my own greatness and the
superlative excellence of my work (some of which I fear I
shall attempt to read,so look out!)

Please allow me to call. Unless I receive definite
intimation that the dogs will be loosed at my advent I shall
assume that you are prepared to endure my company for half-
an-hour;I would probably arrive just after closing time,say
twenty-past-two;for the excellence of M/s Strong's bitter
would detain me at The Sailor's Return until then.

If you prefer to fix time and date yourself (in order to
be sure of being out when I call) please do so,and I will obey
Finally,if I may ask so much,would you acknowledge
reciept of this note,so that I may know you still live at
the address to which this is despatched. I should hate to
come all that way for nothing,although certainly in those
circumstances I should potter up over White Nothe,and take
the air;but White Nothe I have seen before,it is yourself
I want to see.

May I conclude with my good wishes to you,now and
always,whether I see you or no?

Kenneth Hopkins

P.S. Specimen of verse enclosed for your edification,and
may I dare to hope-approbation.

*Kenneth Hopkins' first letter to Llewelyn Powys. This is
the only typewritten letter in the correspondence except
Hopkins' last to Powys.*

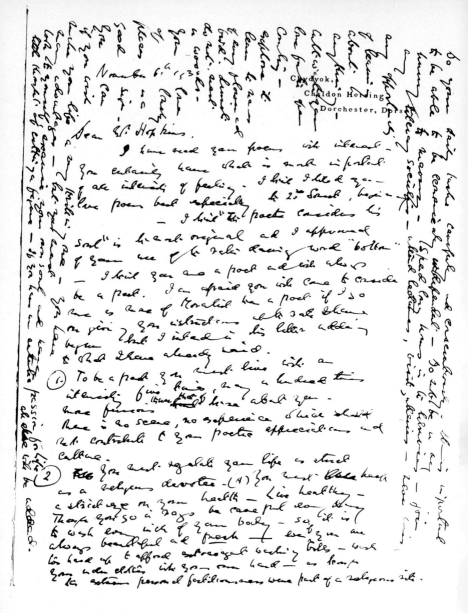

The first page of Llewelyn Powys' first letter to Kenneth Hopkins.

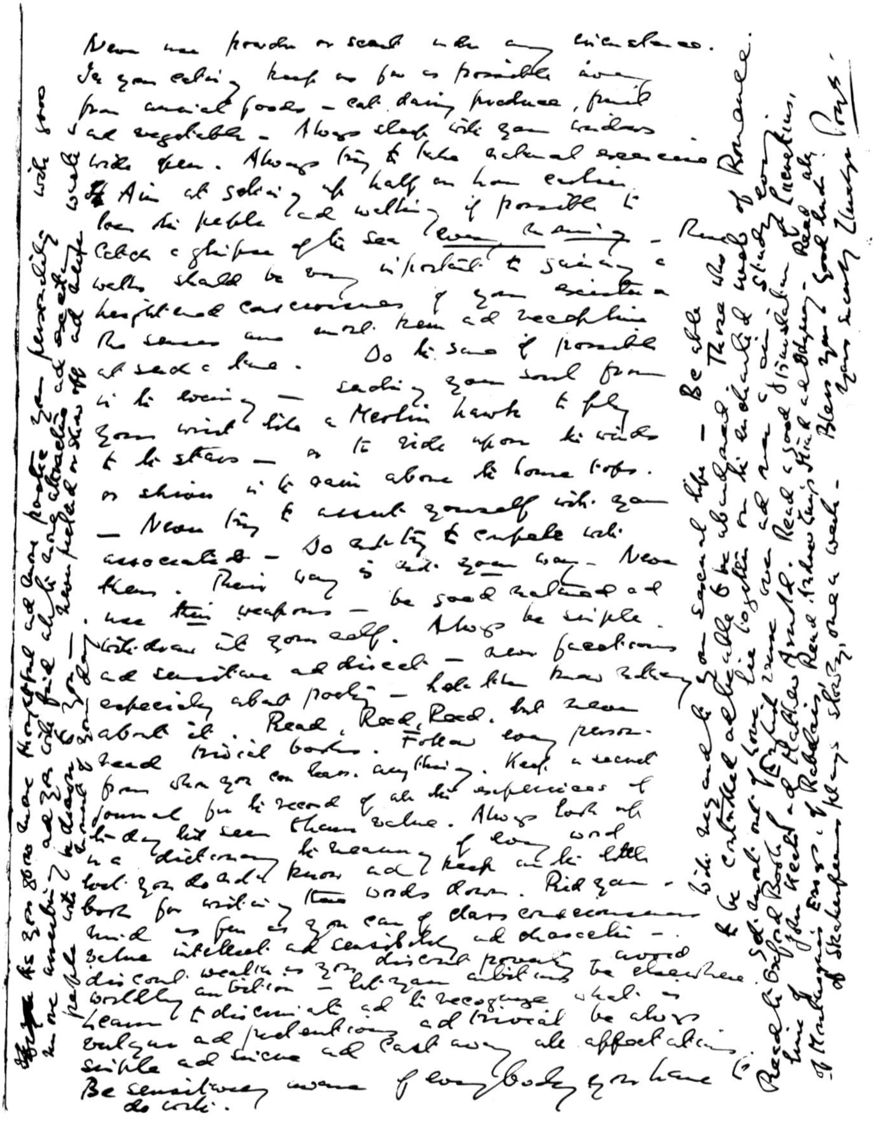

The second page of Powys' first letter to Hopkins.

Llewelyn Powys in 1934.

Kenneth Hopkins in April, 1938.

John Cowper Powys and Kenneth Hopkins, July 25, 1937.

whose merits it is not to refuse a delight offered with an equal admixture of *finesse,* daring, gallantry, and circumspection—a combination rare enough in men to safeguard the virtue of most of their wives and daughters.

LP-10: LLEWELLYN POWYS TO KENNETH HOPKINS

[Postcard:[1]
May 31, 1936]
Thank you for your letter. We will expect you June 14th at 11:30 and I shall be very happy to do what you ask. Thank you for the catalogues but I cant see the book. I shall be interested to see "A Poet's Creed"[2] but I can only promise for myself.

Cerne[3] is a lovely place. Mr. Venn[4] is a man of great charm and character as is his friend Mr Dibben.

Yours sincerely
Llewelyn Powys

---

[1] On the face of the card is a reproduction of Blake's "Simoniac Pope" from the Tate Gallery. Beneath the illustration, in Powys' hand, is one word: "Seducers!"

[2] Probably the 150-line, untitled poem in blank verse dated April 19, 1936, in one of Hopkins' notebooks, which opens:

This is the poem of my present view,

How beauty lives though God has turned his smile.

[3] In *Dorset Essays,* Powys' "Cerne Abbas" chapter pays tribute to the beauty of the village, and takes occasion to comment on morality and Christianity—in describing the great-phallused Cerne Giant cut into white chalk on the hillside overlooking Cerne:

It is strong testimony to the Englishman's good sense that the Cerne Giant on Trendle Hill has been allowed to remain unmutilated throughout the centuries. We can hardly doubt that it has been in serious jeopardy during several periods of our island history, but neither piety, purity, nor prudery has proved strong enough to overcome our English reverence for tradition, for everything that belongs to the past. The terrifying appearance of the Cerne Giant is emphasized by the smallness of his round onion-shaped head and by the hideous spider-like proportions of the crooked limbs, while to over-sensitive observers the figure's "brutish sting" symbolises the final triumph of appetite over intelligence. The chaste reticence of the monks must often have been outraged by

On Sunday, June 14, 1936, Kenneth Hopkins visited
Chydyok—his third meeting with Llewelyn Powys in the
seven and a half months since posting his brash self-invitation.

---

the monster's figure as they looked up to it from the monastery.
Many an honest Puritan must have eyed it askance from under
his broad black hat; and during the decades of Queen Victoria's
reign it must have offered an uncivil affront to the refined sus-
ceptibilities of the ladies and gentlemen, who in comfortable car-
riages smelling of expensive upholstery hot in the sun, rolled
along the dusty roads from Sherborne to Dorchester. . . . It is
strange to consider how this crude affirmation of life, deep dug
in the chalk, overshadowed Aethelmar's Abbey from the day of
its foundation in nine hundred and eighty-seven till the day of its
fall in the sixteenth century, and indeed bids fair to outlast the
dream of grace the cloistered retreat was built to establish.

At the time *Dorset Essays* was published—1935—the Cerne Giant was
to be designated a National Monument.

[4] James Venn owned the Crescent Cottage Bookshop in Weymouth;
William Dibben, formerly his partner, had moved to Bristol. Many
books in Hopkins' growing library (the more important additions
to it are duly recorded in the ledger-journal) came from them; and
often Hopkins noted that James Venn had slipped an extra book,
or two, or three, into the package of purchases. Both booksellers did
much to insure financial success of the volumes of poetry published
the next year by Kenneth Hopkins.

6

Letters: Chaldon Herring
and Bournemouth

June 22, 1936, to November 20, 1936

LP-11: LLEWELYN POWYS TO KENNETH HOPKINS

Chydyok,
Chaldon Herring,
Dorchester, Dorset.
[June 22, 1936]

Midsummer

Dear Mr Kenneth Hopkins

Thank you for your letter—I have read your last volume of poems[1] and was very touched by the inscription and am always arrested by your work—but I do not think I have yet seen a poem of yours that is entirely spontaneous and inspired—but I know that will come, as little by little, your personality developes and you are more and more confident of the paths dedicated to your particular nature. I think you have the intensity and passion of spirit to go far: but learn, learn, learn, from everything and everybody and every circumstance of your life—*Learn to Discriminate*. I liked very much the first of the poems you transcribed by your

---

[1] These little volumes, made for Llewelyn and for John Cowper Powys durings 1936 and 1937, show the young author's care and ingenuity. Fair copies of a dozen or two poems are stapled, glued, or tied between cardboard, then the cardboard was covered with patterned wallpaper—sometimes in contrasting colors in the fashion of three-piece binding. The dust wrappers are tissue, the inscriptions usually in verse.

friend[2]—and if you can manage to bring him to explore the downs with you it would interest me to meet him.

—I have bought two pigeons locally but at present they are locked up. Your shop never answered my inquiries. I suppose the problem of getting quickly to me seemed too great—If you could bring two of the black water turtles you spoke of when you next come I shall be grateful—The middle of next month would do well. The *Rats in the Sacristy* will not be out for a long time—but I will see you have one—

Yours sincerely
Llewelyn Powys

Rats in the Sacristy did not appear until early 1937— with a preface by John Cowper Powys, woodcuts by Gertrude Powys, and a dedication to George Santayana. In the spring of 1936, Llewelyn wrote to John in Wales about his many publishing and writing activities:

> I am getting my *Rats in the Sacristy* together and it should be ready in a month. Nobody will take my *Dorset Essays* in America and in England they still have not sold a 1000 copies. *Damnable Opinions* sold 2000 and have earned me £36 in all. . . . Last year I made £200 by it [writing] but it is always an effort and makes you feel as if the paraffin oil had a hole in the bottom. You have to keep pouring in at the top. I am going to write my *Somerset Essays* though even they do not sell. My *Twelve Months* with Woodcuts by Robert Gibbings can't find a publisher. This is a letter of complaint but a labourer is *worthy of his hire.*

And a letter to Boyne Grainger[3] in New York told of other writings by the bedridden author, and of the hope, "thanks to Van Wyck Brooks' intervention, . . . to get some

---

[2] John Thompson, author of *Three Dawns Ago* (London, 1935), an Australian poet whom Hopkins met through William Dibben.

[3] Boyne Grainger (1882–1962), a friend of Alyse, Llewelyn, and John when they lived in Greenwich Village, wrote two novels, *The Hussy* (1924) and *The Jester's Reign* (1938), both published in New York.

books published in America." (A revised American edition of *Earth Memories* in 1937 carries an introduction by Brooks.) The letter to "Bonnie" closes with the penultimate statement about his eldest brother:

> They have made J. C. P. the
> Bard of the Druid Festival.

LP-12: LLEWELYN POWYS TO KENNETH HOPKINS

[Chydyok
June 29, 1936]

Dear Mr Hopkins,

I never intended that you should buy the Countryman.[1] These papers are usually available in libraries or public reading rooms—I am distressed at your being put to such expense—and I do not at all wish you [to] come by train with the black turtles this is too much—We will let them go for a time as I am stocking my pond with fish from Langport.

I shall be happy to see your friends at August Bank holiday but I must rely on you to see that the visit does not become extended unduly. I can never be persuaded to speak slightingly of Mr Colville[2] for he has given me a wonderful volume of Don Quixote. I think, however, I understand your own reaction and he has taken to every colour of his environment, like a fly on a leaf.

I understand very much your feeling about the bird shop—Do you know Sterne's description of the caged starling[3] in Sentimental Journey? Never bring in appropriate quotations like "slings and arrows of outrageous fortune." This is a public school-schoolmaster's worldly affectation and is unworthy of a well-descended spirit and a little mars

---

[1] The current issue carried an article by Llewelyn Powys.

[2] Unidentified—unless Powys misspelled the name of Keith Coville, another friend of Dibben, who later moved to Australia.

[3] Of the bird—whose English "I can't get out" was useless in France—Sterne later said, "I have borne this poor starling as the crest to my arms." For his crest Llewelyn once said he wanted the dandelion —lowly, but a flower of the sun.

your letter as did the phrase 'contemptuous withal'—Poets
always should express their thoughts with simplicity and
directness—I would like to meet your playmate one day at
the Monmouth Ash. I hope you are happy. It is from a sap-
ling growing out of the original tree.

Yours sincerely
Llewelyn Powys

[Vertically in the margin of page one]

There have been so many people to see lately and so many
more that wish to come that I have had to be very strict
and so as you think of coming in a month's time—we had
better postpone your next visit till then.

LP-13: LLEWELYN POWYS TO KENNETH HOPKINS

[Chydyok
July 8, 1936]

Dear Mr Kenneth Hopkins,
    Thank you for your letter. I was very happy to hear of
your good luck with the Portrait of an Artist.[1] I shall be
interested to know what books you buy.
    —I liked the picture of the ship—You certainly are very
versatile. The fragment of the poem[2] I liked also except
for the words "chancilly" and "despicable." The first I
took exception to as a purist and the second for its "ethical"
connotation. No conversation, no subject should ever be
treated from a moral point of view—they should be judged
intellectually as to whether they are interesting or dull or
aesthetically as to whether they are serious or superficial—
intense or vulgar. Other considerations should be left to
the clergy! It is not that I do not wish to see you before
August—It is a matter of self preservation. I have to see so
many people—and often they are not as careful and considerate as you are about staying too long—I have long come
to regard a sensitive diffidence of this kind as a very test

---

[1] Hopkins paid 6d. for a first edition of *Portrait of the Artist as a
Young Man.*
[2] Unidentified.

as to the delicacy and refinement of a person's nature—
Obtuse people can never all through their lives get it into
their head that they may not be wanted. I have got quite
a number of fish for my pond from Kelvys—I will tell you
about them when you come. I think you are doing well
and will go far—You approach your life with an intensity
that only belongs to imaginative people—I beg you to extend your interests in every direction studying to give your
responses a finer edge. You must read Marcel Proust—This
is important. Moncrieff's translation is splendid.

Yours very sincerely
Llewelyn Powys

[Vertically in the margin of page one, in Alyse Gregory's
hand]

I will lend you my translation of Proust if you can't get
it from the library.

—AG—

KH-5: KENNETH HOPKINS TO LLEWELYN POWYS

125, Southcote Road
Bournemouth.
July 17, 1936

Dear Mr. Powys,

Thank you for your letter. I am sorry to delay my reply
so long.

I have borrowed a typewriter and am trying to collect a
volume of verse to offer publishers. But my difficulty is
this, how to find a title—for "Poems" seeems to me rather
too hackneyed.

In the enclosed poem I have tried to make effective use
of repitition; the phrase "No Second Spring" is rather lovely.
I don't know where it comes from—it is the title of a novel,
but probably is a quotation.[1]

---

[1] The novel *No Second Spring,* by Janet Beith ("Ian Hay's" niece),
was published in 1933. The phrase appears in Ambrose Philips'
"First Pastoral," in 1709, and, earlier still, in "The Bonnie Banks
of Loch Lomond," an anonymous song.

About thirty poems is enough for my book, do you not think? Indeed, I doubt if I have more than that number which I would wish to print. I think I shall send the volume first to J. M. Dent & Co.[2]

I learn from Mr. Venn that Mr. John Cowper is coming to Chaldon; he will find a change very pleasant and to be with you again a great joy—I am afraid he will have many visitors—too many—if this is so, please do not press my request to meet him. Perhaps you will show him my poems and tell him that he has in Bournemouth at least one reader who admires and respects him.

Several of my acquaintences think you *and your brothers* mad!! I do not attempt to argue or defend you, but how I long to make them understand their mistake!—but such people will not understand, and continue belauding popular or best-selling authors in the manner of crowds.

I have recently bought almost nothing except books by yourself or your brothers—not because I intend renouncing all others, but because I wish quickly to acquire a good selection of your books. I now have, altogether, about 25 of them.

A few days ago we caught a large dragon-fly in our store (I mean, where I work). How it got there is a mystery, for it is some miles to the nearest pond where it may have originally lived—but I suppose a dragon fly can travel quite a long way. Also I think it may have come by railway, for our premises abutt on the goods yard.

Well! it is almost ten o'clock and I have yet to go for my first walk today—for I was working till nine.

I hope you are continuing well in this changeable weather —today has been very fine here, and not too warm.

Yours sincerely
Kenneth Hopkins

---

[2] Hopkins' diary entry of August 16, 1936 ("It is long since I wrote herein and of my doings many are hid for I now keep no daily record") tells that Dent rejected the book, but it "now lies with Nelson." In the months ahead, the diary shows, the MS— or a similar one—was also seen and returned by Cobden-Sanderson, Penguin, and Secker; and groups of poems were sent to A. E. Coppard, Maurice Baring, John Trevena, Robert Gibbings, and Sir Edward Marsh.

Love and the Swift Years

Because I likened love to the swift years
And spoke of it as transient, her swift tears
Seemingly flowed from some unfathomed well
And shewed no promise that the tide would break.
I sought for words convincingly to tell
How the swift years tide on to eternity,
And thus—I said the love of you and me.
Then in her eyes I saw the sun awake
Even as I have seen across the sea
Mid driving cruel rain that rift of blue
Which driving the cruel rain lets summer through
And all the birds are glad and sing again.

But even as I reassured her fears
And kissed her eye-lids and her sea-salt tears
Within my heart the seasons' passage seemed
Symbolic of our love—but this I deemed
Too perilous an image to suggest—
It was more true than kind and her sweet breast
Could not receive and bear this certain thing
That our swift love could have no second spring.

LP-14: LLEWELYN POWYS TO KENNETH HOPKINS

[Chydyok]
July 22, 1936

My dear Kenneth Hopkins,
    We liked your poem and Miss Gregory especially liked your repetition of the same words—I liked the burden it carried.

    You must let me know nearer the day of the time of your visit and I will, all being well, arrange that you see my brother J. C. P. for a short visit. But I do this on condition that you promise me you will be *very considerate* of his time and courtesy. My brother is a man of so gentle and generous a disposition that anyone is able to exploit him— and he has a gift of making everybody think they are invaluable to him and he lays himself out utterly to please anyone he likes—so you must behave like that very perfect gentleman the knight in the Canterbury Tales. And you must be very precious of his time—and not after you have met him write to him too often for here again—he is defenceless, being very scrupulous about answering letters[1] and very tender of other people's feelings. I know you will understand my putting all this so clearly. He has a mighty spirit and is far the most exciting human being I have known with an immense store of vital magnetism and I have been jealous of every hour I could spend with him since I reached the age of discretion.

—A friend of mine—an old inhabitant of Montacute— a cultured Baptist and quarry owner died a few months ago at Parkstone and he wished me to have a cactus—His wife has the plant for me. If it were possible for you to call on her and fetch it and later bring it to me on some suitable occasion I should be extremely indebted to you. Mrs. Tavender lives with her sister—They are, I should say, like a band of Pilgrims out of Bunyan! Mrs. H. Tavender—42 Alexandria Road—Upper Parkstone—Dorset.

Yours sincerely
Llewelyn Powys

KH-6: KENNETH HOPKINS TO LLEWELYN POWYS

125, Southcote Road
Bournemouth.
July 23, 1936

Dear Mr. Powys,

Thank you for your letter and enclosure;[1] I will bring your friend's letter when I come to Chaldon. There will be no difficulty about getting the cactus—I will first write and say when I propose collecting it, to avoid finding your friend away from home.

The opportunity of meeting Mr. John Cowper means a great deal to me and I thank you very much for arranging it

[1] Collections of letters by John Cowper Powys at the University of California at Los Angeles, Colgate University, Syracuse University, and the University of Texas, among others, confirm this. It is hard to imagine that anyone in the twentieth century wrote to more people more often than did John Cowper in his ninety years.
[1] Not known.

for me. There are two things I want to ask about my visit: (1) Can you tell me about how long I may stay.—I will then terminate my visit at the right time. I am diffident about remaining too long and should feel embarrassed all the time if I knew not when to leave. The second question is, may I ask him to sign two books: "Wolf Solent" and "Ducdame"— the copies I have of his other books are all rather old and soiled.[2]

LP-15: LLEWELYN POWYS TO KENNETH HOPKINS

[Chydyok,
July 27, 1936]

My dear Kenneth Hopkins,
I have arranged with my brother that you go to him after you have seen me on the morning of August 2nd. I think you might stay half an hour with him and possibly an hour but after half an hour I would be alert for any intimation that you have been long enough and do not allow yourself to be deceived by civil words and all through your life be very jealous lest you stay *too long anywhere* this is an important mark of true courtesy: and always wins approval and appreciation in the great world, and separates you from the uninitiated. Thank you for fetching my rat-tailed cactus. I liked your letter very much—especially your appreciation of the sea fret coming through your window.

Yours sincerely
Llewelyn Powys

KH-7: KENNETH HOPKINS TO LLEWELYN POWYS

125, Southcote Road
Bournemouth.
August 4, 1936

Dear Mr. Powys,
I had no difficulty in finding your brother's home, and when there received a very kind welcome. We were together

---

[2] The remainder of this letter is missing.

almost an hour, and the time passed very swiftly for me, but I remembered your words and I think stayed not too long.

Mr. John Cowper Powys charmed me at once by his courtesy and interest in me. How intensely he lives! All his words and gestures abound with life and vitality and enjoymen of life—but above all I was impressed, as his writings have impressed me—by the depth and power *behind* his thought. I see him now, as I left, standing at the gate shouting directions for my journey, his hair blowing free as I waved good-bye.

It was one of the most memorable occasions of my life. I have asked him to accept a book of my verses, but this I must send on when I have prepared it.

I expect he has now inscribed my books; please thank him again for me, and give him my best wishes ere he returns to Wales.

And you were seemingly better in health, these last times I have seen you. I hope this improvement will remain for the winter months also.

I remained in Chaldon Sunday night, at the Sailor's Return and thought of you much the following morning, but liked not to visit you without notice—I wanted to tell you of my visit to your brother. I returned home by way of Bovington Heath, Wareham, Wimborne, stopping for lunch at Wimborne and reaching home about 3 o'c—one of the happiest week-ends I remember.

Today I secured for 6ᵈ Sir Walter Scott's Lives of The Novelists, Paris, 2 vols. 1825. First Edition, beautifully bound, in good order, an interesting and rather rare book, though of little value. From Mr. Venn on Sunday I got a volume of Peacock containing "Maid Marian" and "Crotchet Castle"—I have not read Peacock up till now—he was awaiting my attention and I finished "Maid Marian" yesterday. Excellent! I now (in Saintsbury's[1] phrase) have "turned Peacockian" and shall buy all his works.

Mr. J. C. P. spoke of Malory's Le Morte D'Arthur!—he has

---

[1] Hopkins still cites George Saintsbury, his students say. Three have written to tell me what advice Kenneth Hopkins gives to young writers—now that he is the age Llewelyn Powys was when he first met him; all have taken his Professional Writing (a course title not to Hopkins' liking, one of his students says) at Southern Illinois University.

All tell of his "write, write, write" advice, and of his belief that it

the same edition as I have read, but alas! do not possess—
a two volume issue of Macmillan's about 1900. (I think). I
read this book many years ago—I mean about seven years—
the prose is magnificent and compares (I think) with anything in English.

I must have left my pyjamas with you in error—I found
them not when bed-time came, but if they are with you I
will collect them when I next see you.

Your socks were really very useful but I managed not to
need the trousers[2]—however, I tried these on, for I fell in
love with their style and colour, but they fitted me ill. I
will bring them when I come.

Naturally I am anxious to get my books, but I feel that
I must let a few weeks pass ere visiting you again; you have
many demands on your time and strength. I will leave you
to fix a date, if you will.

This is a very long letter and now must end.

I send my greetings to Miss Gregory and yourself.

Yours sincerely
Kenneth Hopkins

---

is important for a prose writer to get into print early—with anything. Why not write a murder mystery? he asks them. You may well
be too young to have any great thoughts yet; an action story will
force you to keep moving, to hold the reader's interests, and you
will learn much from seeing your own words in print. (*File for
Death*, by Janet Hart written when she was a sophomore in Hopkins' class, was published in 1965.)

But for young poets—who must hold few hopes of financial success—he strongly counsels the disciplines of the older forms, especially the sonnet. No one should write in free form until he knows
the rules to break, one student writes, and then tells of his continued
perplexity about the first thing Hopkins said to him:

He quietly reads through them (perhaps ten or fifteen poems)
and, after putting out his cigar, came forth with the following
comment: "Well, I won't say whether you are a genius or not,
since genius implies both quantity as well as quality." To this day
I'm still trying to figure out what he meant by that statement. I
haven't had the nerve to ask.

[2] Hopkins, caught in a rainstorm coming back from Rat's Barn—
the farmhouse one mile west of Chydyok where John Cowper lived
from July 5 to August 6—borrowed Llewelyn Powys' socks and
trousers.

The friendship of John Cowper Powys and Kenneth Hopkins lasted over a quarter of a century, until John's death in June, 1963. Several hundred letters document its course, 117 of them from these years before Hopkins enlisted in World War II; I draw on information in the letters (temporarily in my keeping, on loan from Kenneth Hopkins) to fill factual gaps left by the loss of all but two of Hopkins' letters to Llewelyn in Switzerland, but brief quotation cannot suggest the hearty, rambling quality of the exchanges between the old Druid Bard and the eager poetic apprentice forty-two years his junior whom John once called—in a letter to Louise Wilkinson— "that beautiful young letter swallower." The "advice to a young poet" in this correspondence is similar to Llewelyn's only in its active wish to help the young man from Bournemouth. These hundred and more letters from the 'thirties so strongly warrant separate and full publication that I have, for the most part, resisted the urge to quote from them here.

In his first letter to Hopkins, on August 14, 1936, John Cowper Powys wrote:

> How very kind of you it was to do them ["the little book of your poems"] up so well; making quite a bouquet or nosegay . . . their content and manner so fragile and airy and quick *come and gone*, like sad little love-lorn marble-white butterflies on the wing—too quick come and too quick gone. . . . As time goes on I feel sure their author will of necessity summon broader and stronger wings, or even sails. . . .
>
> But do keep and never tear up what you write as the months pass and the years, for there is something in the early verses of youth that no maturity can ever re-capture. . . .
>
> I wonder if you keep any kind of Journal or Diary— Llewelyn's early writings and in one sense *all* his writings were based on his early Diaries.

Less than two years later, in commenting on Penguin's decision to publish Llewelyn's *Ebony and Ivory*, John wrote, "That's fame, my dear Kenneth, that's fame—to be in paper for six pence. Well there *are* cheap editions of the Poets and one day if I live to be ninety I hope to lecture at Bangor University or at least at Bala College on *The Art of K. Hopkins.*" And he told Kenneth that he had included half of a Hopkins sonnet in his chapter on Proust in *The Pleasures of Literature* (London, 1938) —changed for a more westerly audience to *Enjoyment of Literature* (New York, 1938). With more enthusiasm than shire accuracy, John Cowper wrote that after reading Proust—"from an Anglo-Celtic point of view so comically devoid of all impulses of magnaminity towards the object of desire"—the reader begins "to sigh for that more indulgent, more generous, less analytical touch of—Well! say of the sonnets of Shakespeare, a touch which can still be found in the poetry of as young a poet as our Dorsetshire Kenneth Hopkins."

John Cowper Powys died at age ninety, and although there is no record of a Powys-on-Hopkins lecture at Bangor, or Bala, he did attain paper-book publication in 1965 when Penguin issued his *Wolf Solent*—at ten shillings sixpence. And this is the Dedication of Hopkins' *English Poetry: A Short History* published in 1962, the year before John's death:

> To walk erect for nearly ninety years
> Nor tread one creature down, nor crush one flower;
> To see the heart of things, and still find hope;
> To endure the thorn and gain the scent of furze,
> ('He deserves not sweet that will not taste of sour') ;
> To stride towards that for which the cautious grope;
> To know all knowledge leaves all truth unknown;
>
> To perceive the marvellous dignity of a stone;
> To give all life, and every inanimate thing

Pity and countenance, and the loan of strength
To those that long sustain the burning day:
This he has shown me, and for this I bring
Old wise John Cowper Powys honour at length
To mark a debt else more than I can pay.

In his diary entry for August 16, 1936, Hopkins wrote a single sentence about their first meeting: "I have met J. C. Powys and conversed with him upwards of an hour on Malory and James Joyce, also other matters." Not until November 14 does he make the next entry, and then to tell of Llewelyn's physical relapse and slow recovery.

LP-16: LLEWELYN POWYS TO KENNETH HOPKINS

[Chydyok,
August 15, 1936]

Dear Mr Kenneth Hopkins,
    It was very good of you to remember my birthday—but I cannot be persuaded to share your enthusiasm for the poem[1] you sent me. It is very good of its kind—but it is not *really first rate.*

    It is kind of you to suggest the Wordsworth but although I admire *this* poet very much I have a serviceable copy—but it was good of you to think of me in this connection. I hope you all will have a very happy holiday.
                                Yours sincerely
                                Llewelyn Powys

KH-8: KENNETH HOPKINS TO LLEWELYN POWYS

125, Southcote Road
Bournemouth.
August 29, 1936

Dear Mr. Powys,
    I wonder if it will be possible for me to visit you once more before you are obliged to leave your little house in the

[1] *Ballad of the White Horse,* by G. K. Chesterton—a "fine" edition by Methuen with illustrations by John Austen.

garden—as, I suppose, you soon must, for Autumn is very near.

I have had a very generous and appreciative letter from Mr. J. C. Powys about the poems I sent him—mostly short love poems like the one I enclose with this letter. He urges me, even as you did, to keep a journal, and I have explained that I do so, following the suggestion you made to me almost a year ago.

I am collecting first editions of J. E. Flecker; I am convinced that he will come more and more to be regarded as a very great poet, and if for no other reason than as an investment, his books should be worth having—but I buy to keep, not to sell.

I have undertaken to purchase a small mahogany bookcase, something like this: [sketch] in which I shall keep all books by yourself and brothers, etc.—I now have about 25 all told. I think [Philippa Powys'] "The Blackthorn Winter" very fine, it is written so poetically and sensitively.

I enclose also a reproduction of the title page of a book I have for you (I have a copy for myself also), it seems a fairly common book, but very interesting. I hope you have not seen it before.

I hope you are well, and Miss Gregory also; personally, I find the very hot days rather trying—I get headaches, and much prefer Autumn and Winter.

Yours sincerely
Kenneth Hopkins

[Enclosures]

Song

Swiftly, swiftly, laughing one!
All the hills are wet with dew
Sparkling in the morning sun;
Swiftly, swiftly, swiftly come!

Kindly heart, my gentle one,
Evening treads the hills at last,
And the hours of joy are past,
And the time of tears is come.

Kenneth Hopkins

ENGLAND DELINEATED
or, a
GEOGRAPHICAL DESCRIPTION
of every county in
ENGLAND AND WALES
with a concise account of
its most important products,
natural and artificial.

For the Use of Young Persons.

with outline maps of all counties

———

FIFTH EDITION
considerably improved

———

Such noble warlike steeds, such herds of kine,
So sleek, so vast; such spacious flocks of sheep,
What other paradise adorn but thine,
Britannia? . . . .
. . . . . To these thy naval streams
Thy frequent towns superb of busy trade
And ports magnific add, and stately ships
Innumerous.

Dyer's Fleece
LONDON:
Printed for J. Johnson, St. Paul's Churchyard
By J. Bensley, Bolt Court, Fleet Street
1803.

LP-17: LLEWELYN POWYS TO KENNETH HOPKINS

Chaldon Herring
Dorchester, Dorset
August 31, [1936]

My dear Kenneth Hopkins,

Thank you for your letter and poem. I liked it very much. It was simple natural and true—and had in it sad music.

If I may say so I think Flecker and Chesterton and Rupert Brooke and that American war poet they make so much of all good but I cannot believe deserve the high position they hold at present. I would like your taste to become severer and more exacting. Could you perhaps arrange your next visit to take place any day after the middle of this month—only be sure to let us know when we are to expect you. I have acquired a beautiful small copy of the "Prince" to lend you if you have not yet read it. Miss Gregory saved the life of a hedgehog a few days ago. He had been swimming round and round in our pond with only his nose protruding and could not get out. Yesterday I looked at the pollen of the sunflower in my microscope—like lovely golden frog-spawn—and I seemed to take it as a sure token of life's strange beauty—coin of reassurance—and the male organ of a male bumble bee carried the same message.

Yours sincerely

Llewelyn Powys

KH-9: KENNETH HOPKINS TO LLEWELYN POWYS

125, Southcote Road

Bournemouth.

September 6, 1936

Dear Mr. Powys,

I am unable to come to Chaldon after the 13th—next Sunday—until the first week in October; if the 13th is too soon please let me know—it is really a little before the time you suggest—but if I may come I shall expect no reply to this letter.

Thank you for the offer of "The Prince"—I shall be glad to borrow it. I have never yet read it. Also I would like Proust which Miss Gregory offered me.

This must be a brief letter, but I enclose a new poem.

Yours sincerely

Kenneth Hopkins

P.S. If I come on Sunday it will be soon after 11:00.

P.T.O.

I forgot to tell you that I have asked Boots Libraries [of Boots the Chemist] to send you a catalogue of second-hand books. There are many bargains in it. I have selected a book of woodcuts by Robert Gibbings, and your own "Earth Memories." If you care to have books sent to Bournemouth Branch there will be no postage to pay and I can bring them to you.

K.H.

LP-18: LLEWELYN POWYS TO KENNETH HOPKINS

[Postcard:
Chydyok,
September 7, 1936]

We will be very happy to see you next Sunday unless I send word to the contrary. I liked your poem very much except the expression "Slumberous June"[1] which is too cloying a word I think—and one I would always avoid especially in this context.

Yours sincerely
Llewelyn Powys

This visit, however, which would have been their fifth (not counting the day that Hopkins delivered the rattailed cactus, on which there was no conversation) did not take place. On the scheduled Sunday, September 13, Powys had another severe hemorrhage. But his health must have declined in the days before; Hopkins' letter of Tuesday, September 8, asking Alyse Gregory to send news of her husband's health the next week, implies that she had already canceled the visit. All told, the time Kenneth Hopkins and Llewelyn Powys had spent together was somewhat less than five hours. They never met again.

KH-10: KENNETH HOPKINS TO ALYSE GREGORY

125, Southcote Road
Bournemouth
September 8, 1936

Dear Miss Gregory,

I enclose three books and will keep a little longer, if I may, "The Prince." Please thank Mr. Powys on my behalf for the loan of these books.

---

[1] In "The Shadows and Lights of Love"; Hopkins changed the line to read, "Where the shadowy trees cast their shadows in langorous June."

Deloney[1] pleases me greatly: I shall as soon as possible obtain his works myself.

Did I tell you I have news of a copy of "Wood and Stone,"[2] which I have sought so long? I go to Winchester during the week-end to secure it.

I am sorry Mr. Powys is so ill; I hoped to hear better news of him this time. Please let me know again next week how he is.

The little boys of Bournemouth now have their first supplies of fireworks and may be heard discharging the $\frac{1}{2}^d$ monsters anytime after six o'clock—I find it annoying—yet as a child I did the same, so now suffer what my elders did and try to be patient!

I like the description of the Ballad Makers in Introduction to Deloney: "Who be more bawdie than they? Who uncleaner than they? Who more licentious and loose-minded?"

Yours sincerely

Kenneth Hopkins

------

[1] Earlier in 1936, in a chapter on Thomas Deloney for *Rats in the Sacristy*, Llewelyn Powys wrote:

It has been a fanciful prejudice with me to remark a difference between flower-shop salesmen and ironmongers. The former, because it is their profession to make commercial profit out of beauty, grow, so it seems, shallow and artificial in their address, whereas ironmongers, because it is their business to supply people with utensils necessary for daily use, become sensible and honest citizens. Thomas Deloney may be said to represent the ironmongers in literature; one who knows how essential colanders, kettles, frying-pans, and saucepans are to human beings. The unredeemed lives of ordinary people are his province. . . . at once these phantom puppets of his imagination are walking between the street booths, standing at their cutting-stools, or sitting at their removable refectory tables gutting pudding pies; are actually there before us, at one moment out of temper, and at the next grinning, but always there firmly set in farting flesh. No lover of the sun should be content to remain unacquainted with the prose works of this master. . . . Deloney wrote with the enfranchisement of one of the lower classes too pressed by life's realities to trouble much about its niceties.

[2] John Cowper Powys' first novel (New York, 1915; London, 1917).

AG-5: ALYSE GREGORY TO KENNETH HOPKINS

Chydyok,
Chaldon Herring,
Dorchester, Dorset.
September 25, 1936

Dear Mr. Hopkins,

Mr. Powys had a rather serious hemorrhage of the lungs on Sunday owing to having seen too many people and is unable to write any letters, and is, indeed, very ill. But he read your letter and is pleased to know that you have been enjoying your holiday. He would prefer to have his own annotated copy of Lucretius back—I think this continued damp weather is exceptionally dangerous for anyone with any trouble of the lungs.

Sincerely yours,
Alyse Gregory

[Vertically in the margin]

We both think it is wonderful how much you get from your life—how much ardour you put into your days.

KH-11: KENNETH HOPKINS TO LLEWELYN POWYS

125, Southcote Road
Bournemouth.
October 4, 1936

Dear Mr. Powys,

I hope I may hear soon that you are better in health once again; your recent increase of illness alarmed me, for you seemed so well.

I send you a little book of poems, the best of what I have written this year, I think. Many of them you have seen, but you may care to have them all bound up together.

I have just secured that splendid edition of Le Morte D'arthur issued by Macmillan in 1900, two volumes. Your brother, Mr. J. C. Powys has the same edition; it is the best I know, except one published recently at £10..10s!

I look forward to when we may meet again, but I expect this must be many weeks hence. Autumn is beginning to visit the woods, and soon I shall be happy, for more than any I love the afternoons of late October and sunset over the moors, with bracken turned to bronze, and the light behind the pines.

The fearless sparrows now come daily right into our warehouse and perch everywhere, even on the moving motorlorries! They carry away great whisps of straw, and play games of chasing among the roof-joists.

You must not try to write to me if you are still very unwell, but perhaps Miss Gregory will let me know how you are progressing.

I send my best wishes to her and to yourself.

Yours sincerely
Kenneth Hopkins

Postscript to my letter enclosed [on a separate sheet].

Dear Mr. Powys,

I have thought a lot whether to send you my Collected Satires or not—and here they are.

Much of the contents (I think) will displease you, much you will think silly. As I read the poems,[1] I see a lot of stuff I should never show you, if it were not in the book, but there is here collected quite a mass of stuff in a style not represented in my previous poems sent to you.

Many of my views have changed since I have known you, and especially since I have read "Impassioned Clay."[2] Probably never again shall I write as in some of these poems, but they are a stage in my development and as such need, I suppose, no apology.

Kenneth Hopkins

---

[1] At the end of another notebook of poems written in 1936 Hopkins wrote, "I was very fond of satire, but in its practice pretty incompetent; in 1935 I collected all my satires in one book, which I still have [now at the University of Texas], and I have copied below a few specimens." These lines are from "Men Call it Love":

> Eyes once so clear with film of age oerclouded;
> Skin once so white with sticky paints enshrouded . . .
> The sagging breasts, the drooping eyelids see,
> In years so young, so old in harlotry.

[2] Kenneth Hopkins has said recently that this book remains his key to Llewelyn Powys' thought. The copy given to him by Powys is the original American edition with the woodcut by Lynd Ward, which Longmans omitted from the later English edition.

AG-6: ALYSE GREGORY TO KENNETH HOPKINS

[Chydyok]
October 8, 1936

Dear Mr. Hopkins,

My husband is still too ill to write any letters,[1] but wants me to thank you for the book of poems so beautifully written and bound together. He will write you of it when he is able.

I wonder whether you would very much mind posting back the Deloney, if possible by return, as I have to look up a quotation in it to verify for a book of my husband's now at the printers—And perhaps at the same time you could put in my husband's copy of Lucretius,[2] since you now have another, and he particularly prizes it—indeed it is much coveted by many young admirers of his.

What wonderful acumen you have in searching out valuable books. If you enjoy the autumn you ought to delight in these clear sunsets.

Sincerely yours,
Alyse Gregory

LP-19: LLEWELYN POWYS TO KENNETH HOPKINS

[Chydyok
October 8, 1936]

Dear Kenneth Hopkins,

I was very happy to receive your book of poems arranged with such care—Many of them I took great pleasure in reading and I thank you for your delightful gift. I am afraid we

---

[1] But Llewelyn Powys did write, on the same day; his letter follows. It has, however—as do the next three letters, his last from England—a summary and valedictory tone that he had used before, when very ill, and would use in Switzerland during the last months of his life in letters written to many friends.

[2] Kenneth Hopkins had bought an identical edition—the Cyril Bailey translation (Oxford: The Clarendon Press, 1910)—and asked if he could trade it for Llewelyn's annotated copy.

must not expect to have a meeting for a long time—This last attack has been a serious one and it is important for me to keep as quiet as I can. In the meanwhile—you must remember all I have told you, and live every moment of your life with passionate intensity—reading, reading, reading—and clearing up all obscure passages so that you leave nothing behind *ununderstood.*

Now as I have constituted myself as a kind of Lord Chesterfield writing to his nephew—I will venture to give you a few more hints in the matter of civilities. By becoming a poet you enter the society of the most select company possible and your sensitive consideration for other people should be very responsive.

It was charming of you to flatter me with the deference of the old-fashioned title "Sir"—but I think you would do better still to address me as Mr Powys—and study to show your concern and respect in other ways. For example it was teasing to me when you so casually tried to possess yourself of my Lucretius—full of so many intimate notes which was lent to you as an especial favour—It was teasing to me when you told me that you had "tried my trousers on"—that kind of familiar facetiousness of tone is all right with friends of your own age but unsuitable when adopted towards an older person. It has the same note of poor taste as your first letter, or as pressing to know my brother Theodore. These are all very little faults but they indicate a kind of precocity—that you should be careful to avoid. You cant be too reserved when you approach anything that is personal—You must try to master all secrets of good breeding. This is very important. Keats used to say every gentleman is my natural enemy[1]—but it is foolish for every true poet is of necessity more gentle bred than the most courteous gentleman—You must give some attention to these subtle points.

Yours sincerely
Llewelyn Powys

---

[1] "Keats, being a little too sensitive on the score of his origin, felt inclined to see in every man of birth a sort of natural enemy"—from Chapter 16 of Leigh Hunt's *Autobiography*. I am indebted to Walter Jackson Bate for identifying this quotation.

KH-12: KENNETH HOPKINS TO LLEWELYN POWYS

125, Southcote Road
Bournemouth.
October 11, 1936

Dear Mr. Powys,

Thank you for your letter; I am glad you wrote as you did, and I will try to remember your advice.

I am sure you do not think in any of these points that I erred through anything but forgetfulness of that restraint you so rightly expect. I live most of my life among gross insensitive people; it is difficult always to avoid being tainted. Please do not think I am excusing myself, but I think this might explain it.

I have just read "The Cradle of God,"[1] and liked it greatly—more than I expected, for a book on the subject by another writer would not attract me at all. As it is, I was deeply interested all through as you recount the story of the Jews: I wish I could visit an Oxford Group meeting and read the passage on page 305 which begins "Even in the hour of death, upon the threshold of the grave, I would not hesitate to speak out what is in my mind."[2] Half the young people at these meetings are attracted more by the personalities of the preachers than by their doctrines, espe-

---

[1] This longest of Powys' books offers many contrasts: a history of the people of the Old Testament and their need for a god, it was written in eight weeks on the Isle of Capri in 1929; dedicated to his cousin, the Reverend John Hamilton Cowper Johnson, the book includes a two-page epigraph from Rabelais, and this last sentence:

Christianity is but a single radiant eddy in that deep dark stream of shadow and sunshine which bears us along together, plants and beasts and men, towards the engulfing ocean of an unfathomable and unintelligible eternity.

[2] And continues: "I would have no boy or girl turn from the earth. . . . Have care, O heathen youth! These matters remain unproven. Let not the free action of your mind, be impeded or checked by the resonant intoning of priests, as they walk in procession, dressed in lace. . . . Be generous, be free, be impassioned, be *understanding*. . . . Even now your hour passes. With ineluctable glee dip your hands deep into the salt fresh sea of life. Lift up your eyes and behold the sun."

cially the young girls, who do not realize that to sacrifice themselves spiritually is quite as sexual an action as to do so bodily. They would not have this hysterical devotion for preachers, old and angular, with ugly, misshapen bodies! I know girls now, with young clean bodies, and in their hearts a yearning for something no Oxford Meeting will give them, who flutter from group to group and church to church, following some smug young parson who will never satisfy their desires.

Do you know that line of Dryden: "What has been, has been, and I have had my hour."[3] It is a favourite of mine. Some of the girls and boys will live and never have their hour, never guess that life is sweeter without the dominence of these hysterical "confessions" and "witnesses." O, I hate such despicable philanderings!

I hope the Deloney arrived on time; I shall seek a copy for myself, and am glad you told me of him.

I send greetings to Miss Gregory.

Yours sincerely
Kenneth Hopkins

LP-20: LLEWELYN POWYS TO KENNETH HOPKINS

[Chydyok
October 13, 1936]

My dear Kenneth Hopkins,

I was very glad to get your letter and to know that you had not been offended by my complaints. I think we all ought to learn to weave endless circles round[1] the personalities of each new mortal sprite we encounter—We should never take anything for granted after the fashion of un-

---

[3] "Translations from Horace: The Twenty-ninth Ode of the Third Book," stanza viii.

[1] The last lines of Coleridge's "Kubla Khan":

> And all should cry, Beware! Beware!
> His flashing eyes, his floating hair!
> Weave a circle round him thrice,
> And close your eyes with holy dread,
> For he on honeydew hath fed,
> And drunk the milk of Paradise.

abashed commercial travellers but should cultivate the diffidence of stately mandarins and let our nodding heads be
packed with far-fetched hesitations and considerations. I
will initiate you into these subtle secrets. Do try to get hold
of Lord Chesterfield's letters—They will advise you. I am
still too ill to write—but I wished to send this greeting.

Your sincere,
Llewelyn Powys

LP-21: LLEWELYN POWYS TO KENNETH HOPKINS

[Chydyok,
November 9, 1936]

Dear Kenneth Hopkins,
I was very glad to get your letter and commend you much
for your candour over the "Prince"—this is often difficult
but if ever there is an excuse for strict honesty it is in matters of one's personal taste in literature. Your poem also I
liked, it is light but it is good. I must thank you also for the
old photograph which I am glad to have. I was interested
to hear that your mother came from Tintinhull—I used
often to go there as a boy, especially with my brother J. C. P.
We were very fond of the village. There was I remember
a Doctor at Martock calld Adams.[1] I still have to be very
careful and keep quiet but I am very much better and still
hope to go to Switzerland in December if I get through
without any more setbacks.

Yours sincerely
Llewelyn Powys

[Vertically in the margin]

I deeply envied you that walk in the moonlight—Such an
experience carries with it more wisdom than many books—
You were then not only abroad in Ringwood[2] but in the
Abyss of the Cosmos

---

[1] Hopkins' mother's maiden name, but there was no connection.
Tintinhull and Martock are several miles northwest of Montacute.
[2] A small town north of Bournemouth, on the edge of the New
Forest.

LP-22: LLEWELYN POWYS TO KENNETH HOPKINS

Chydyok,
Chaldon Herring,
Dorchester, Dorset.
[November 20, 1936]

Dear Kenneth Hopkins,

Thank you for your letter. Think no more of Lucretius or of the precipitate visit—I made more of these matters than they deserved out of my affection for you and wanting you to be a very beloved poet, beyond criticism of every kind. Of course I shall be delighted if you meet my brother[1] through Mr Venn's good offices. I should get and study Lord Chesterfield's letters—All the young men of fashion at the beginning of the 19th century modelled their behaviour upon them—and their wit, sense and smooth knowledge of the world and its ways—and insight into social relationships are most valuable. Johnson said they presented the "morals of a whore and the manners of a dancing master"[2] but he did not understand matters of behaviour. Have you read Boswell's Life?—You certainly should study this carefully.

Would you present my compliments to your mother and thank her very much for her most generous offer of hospitality—One day if I get well I would like to pay you a visit but as long as my health is precarious I find visiting a difficulty—so you must think no more of this.

I enjoyed your poem and it was good of you to copy it out for me—I still do not think it represents the best you

---

[1] T. F. Powys. Although they had twice exchanged words, Kenneth Hopkins still had not *met* him.

[2] Boswell assigns the remark to 1754; he records these words by Johnson in 1776: "Lord Chesterfield's *Letters to his Son,* I think, might be made a very pretty book. Take out the immorality, and it should be put into the hands of every young gentleman. An elegant manner and easiness of behaviour are acquired gradually and imperceptibly. . . . we are all less restrained than women. Were a woman sitting in company to put out her legs as most men do, we should be tempted to kick them in. . . . Every man of any education would rather be called a rascal, than accused of deficiency in *the graces.*"

could do—It is as though your imagination cannot yet find free expression—Your poems are good—but not sufficiently arresting. They do not as yet separate you absolutely from the ordinary world; and yet they are obviously written by a poet, by an immature Kit Marlowe. I am glad you have read Ernest Dowson. You should study all his poems. I think you should try to end the Dance of Love with the lines

> "This exquisite delight that I may share
> The Happiness of Gods."

> "O my love,
> Our happiness was builded for this!"

is in my opinion too didactic philosophic—You must always try to detach your own sensations pure and naked—like leaping fish—from the welter of traditional sensations and to express them. As I have told you before keep diaries, journals, note books and never waste an hour of your life, no not a moment—and become more and more Discriminating.

Yours sincerely.
Llewelyn Powys

On December 2, 1936, three years to the day before his death, Llewelyn Powys left England forever.

7

Letters: Davos Platz
and Bournemouth
December 17, 1936, to April 6, 1938

LP-23: LLEWELYN POWYS TO KENNETH
HOPKINS

> Clavadel
> Davos Platz
> Switzerland.
> December 17, 1936

Dear Kenneth Hopkins,

   Thank you for your letter—I liked the poems especially the two shorter poems; though they read remote as though almost they were translations.

> How the bird-flight of love
> Darts across my heart![1]

These lines especially pleased me.

   We got here safely in good order—and I have since been

---

[1] The poem is in *Collected Poems: 1935–1965*:

> ### O Love Not Transient Things
>
> O love not transient things!
> Our life, sad setting of day,
> The beauty of women, these
> Fade and are nothing, love them not!
>
> How the bird-flight of love
> Darts across my heart!
>
> "O beautiful!" I cry—
> But it is gone.

143

in bed getting used to rarefied air. We spent a week first at Lausanne looking out upon the lake. A friend of ours sent a very swift comfortable car to convey us to Bournemouth Central and as we swept down the Street towards the Station Miss Gregory caught sight of you on a bicycle but before I could give you my blessing we had gone too far.

I am very sorry about the abdication—It is a great shame —and the speech of the Archbishop I thought very sentimental—and I can well understand how any abandonment of the pomps and vanity of this world would present itself as "a tragedy" to so old a courtier.[2]

It is strange to look out of the windows at these old scenes—The village remains wonderfully unaltered—and I can make out the very place where I came over the mountains opposite from Arosa—giving myself a haemorrhage as soon as ever I rested my head upon the pillow in the little mountain inn.

The twilights of the morning and evening have an abstract quality, light as the inside of a mother of pearl shell flushed with a rose colour. A sparrow, a cole-tit, a great-tit come to the balcony for food—We are very happily placed here in a little house with no one but ourselves to be entertained—

I do hope you will have a happy Christmas. Read, Read, Read. Learn, learn, learn; meditate, meditate, meditate: LIVE, LIVE, LIVE—but above all sink always into yourself for it is from within our own gates that we are able to start upon our adventuring most fortunately—

Yours sincerely
Llewelyn Powys

---

[2] John Cowper Powys also wrote to Kenneth the week after Edward VIII's abdication, but his concern was with the temporal, rather than with the spiritual leader:

What a sad day this is with the Roundheads victorious! There is something curiously teasing about this Island's history being lost, submerged, dominated, puritanized under the "mandates" of these smug Colonial Premiers. Well I would like to have a talk with brother Llewelyn on "thik little job."

At Clavadel, a very small village two miles south of Davos Platz, the Powyses lived at the home of Lisaly Gujer whom he had met in 1912 when he collapsed after the solitary trek over the Furka Pass from Arosa. Llewelyn stayed in bed for only a few weeks; his temperature dropped almost on arrival and he reported having a "famous appetite"—but this was not an unmixed good, because of his proneness to the recurrent gastric troubles that plagued several of his family.

At Bournemouth, early in December, Kenneth Hopkins' old problem of joblessness was back. On the 11th of December his journal records a letter to Weymouth, applying for a job with a builders' material firm nearer to the other Powyses, James Venn, and his new group of friends. (And, at that time, Llewelyn's return was assumed; he continued to rent Chydyok.) "Have few ties in Bournemouth," the journal says, "only Paul [French]." Then, two days later, "A woeful thing has befallen," and, as he did in his first letter to Llewelyn, he cloaked his feelings with arch words:

> I cease not to bewail, it is this, I am thrust out of employment. Dolorous do I find the lack of monies paid to me weekly now not so paid. Though in truth, not to labour daily giveth my soul certain balm which must be healing though transitory.

The following page shows a list of pubs stayed at during a holiday trip to "Hants, Berks, Wilts, and Oxon"—and the next entry tells in four lines of his New Year's Eve:

> Walked along the front alone 11:00-11:45. Helped a wounded seabird to shelter and found a large green glass ball. ?—a bomb? Think not. Home 1:00, very wet of rain and spray.

LP-24: LLEWELYN POWYS TO KENNETH HOPKINS

The last day of
the Year *1936*.

Clavadel
Davos Platz
Switzerland
[January 1, 1937][1]

Dear Mr Kenneth Hopkins,

Your letter reached me last night and I was sorry to hear its news. I hope you will not be inconvenienced for long. I think if you had read "The Prince" *to the end* this would have never happened. You must have been stupid and allowed your nervous self assertiveness to have trespassed and not had the wit by civilities and ironic submissions (which cost nothing) to placate your enemy—No intelligent person would have allowed anyone capable of doing you so great a mischief to have gone unplacated. Lord Chesterfield's letters would have taught you this. I would like to hear the real truth of the trouble. Were you indolent? Were you cheeky? Were you caught with your fingers in the till? Or were you foolish enough to show *real thoughts* or more dangerous still your antinomianism? I cannot tell—but I would like to know the exact details and so will be better able to advise and judge.

I suppose you do not think of trying to make a living elsewhere or travelling to London with a shilling in your pocket as Johnson did with Garrick! Are you prepared to take *any* job *anywhere* or will you wait for an opening to come in Bournemouth? If you like I would write to Mr Aish the old octogenarian electrical master who remembers my grandfather at Stalbridge? I also might have some influence with Mr Athelstan Rendale though like most well-

---

[1] The Swiss method of postmarking follows the European system—the day first, then the month and year—but, because the post office at Clavadel used sansserif Roman numerals for the month, two letters in the English edition of *Advice to a Young Poet* are out of order. Bodley Head numbers XXXIX and XLIII should be February 10, 1938 ("10.11.38") and February 6, 1939 ("6.11.39") rather than November 10, 1938, and June 11, 1939. Their numbering and mine, however, do not coincide after Llewelyn's eighth letter because of the additional letters included here.

to-do business men he is very shrewd and would not be likely to employ you in any capacity unless you could prove you would be useful—but I might try and you might manage some subordinate position in his office or become a doorkeeper? Let me know what you think you could do? Could you be a clerk? Are you good at figures? Let me know what you think of this?

Your idea of my "planting" your poems in the Daily Herald would be no use, even if I were in a position to do such a thing—It might be feasible if you had written something they were likely to accept but I do not think you have. You must send out your poems to magazines—Look at the back of your Writers Year Book and you will see which papers accept verse! Try sending a poem about our coast to the Dorset Echo or about the New Forest to a Bournemouth paper. In any case make the most of your free time, read, read, read, take notes, frequent libraries, picture galleries, museums—interest yourself in every branch of knowledge—visit old buildings, cultivate your sensibility with regard to architecture—I think it is probably best to stay in Bournemouth where you have a home behind you—but let me hear your plans and know what happens.

I hope you will have a happy New Year.

Yours sincerely
Llewelyn Powys

The word "planting," as Llewelyn Powys used it, has stronger connotations than perhaps he realized. Hopkins had asked whether it would be feasible for Powys to forward several signed poems to the editor who had been buying his essays; "sponsor" would seem the fairer term. But Hopkins had been having mixed reactions to his poetry; over a span of a few days the journal records that William Dibben decided not to go through with his plan of giving a collection to C. Day Lewis; that A. E. Coppard sent back eleven poems with "comments and criticisms"; that Maurice Baring "writes briefly, being ill, but with enthusiasm" about the twelve poems sent to him; and, on January 6, that he had, "a day or two ago, a highly characteristic letter of Llewelyn re. my unemployment. (No.—)

Have replied and expect to hear about next Monday."
This is the first indication that Hopkins has been carefully saving and numbering—or someday plans to number—his letters from Powys, a care much rarer in 1937
than in 1969; somewhat later John Cowper Powys wrote
to Louis Wilkinson about Hopkins' suggestion that
J. C. P.'s letters be published: "The interest of this young
Mr. H is as you might say *touching* in these Cynical Days."

Hopkins, as he had done a year earlier when out of
work, became much more active in his literary pursuits.
After noting that Johnson wrote *Rasselas* in one week, he
wrote four poems, "72 lines, in half an hour." His book
purchasing—or at least the recording of it—increased.
Many are first editions, but the prices average four shillings
and rarely exceed six; his purchases early in 1937 include
books by James Hanley, Edward Thomas, Masefield,
yet another Lucretius, Robert Green, Whyte-Melville,
Stephen Vincent Benét, "Omar Khayam—1st Ed? ! — I
don't think!" Besant, Henry Kingsley, Swinburne, Walter
Raleigh (*Style*), Leacock, Burns, *Gil Blas, Spectator*—8
vols., Cowper—8 Vols., F. M. Hueffer, Gibbons, Trevena,
Mr. Weston's Good Wine, and some dozen more. But the
major decision was made the first week in January:

> My first printed book is in the press, a pamphlet called
> "Twelve Poems," ready in about a month. [Albert] Page, of
> Charminster Road, is printing 50 copies at a cost of
> (about) £1.

The print order was increased the next week:

> The book "Twelve Poems" progresses: four poems are now
> printed. I have just seen Page (printer). We discussed the
> covers, etc. I have cut the pages for covers (25 blue, first
> issue, signed) and 80 green (ordinary issue) and this is now
> in my trouser-press to flatten!

A light touch was added:

> I have written a review of "Twelve Poems" which I hope
> to get printed, it is by "Christopher Adams"—I do hope it is
> printed, what a merry jest!

And by January 31—two weeks after publication—the first
returns were in:

> "12 Poems" has sold well—progress may be seen at the end
> of this book. I have now entered [the names of purchasers
> and donees] as far as Robert Gibbings, to whom yesterday
> I sent a copy. Llewelyn writes appreciatively and JC. also.
> Dibben likes the book title—I can understand why.

The tally on the inside back cover of the journal shows
forty-four copies distributed—seventeen of them with the
compliments of the author. Expenses were £3..14..6 and
income £2..12..6 (the price was one shilling sixpence, but
both Canon Marsh and the Reverend Lewin seem to have
added a subvention). Creeping costs and complimentary
copies were little foxes, but in February William Dibben
took thirty-one copies for his bookshop (on account),
two more copies were sold (and three more given away),
and Hopkins' final accounting shows—*if* there were no
bookstore returns and no "bad pay" among his debtors—
a one-shilling profit from the publication of "Twelve
Poems."

LP-25: LLEWELYN POWYS TO KENNETH HOPKINS

Clavadel
Davos Platz
Switzerland.
January [29], 1937

Dear Kenneth Hopkins,
    It was a great pleasure to me to receive your little volume
so excellently printed by Mr Albert Page—I congratulate

you and hope it will be the beginning of an adventurous
literary career. They surely possess a scrannel[1] note light
and charming as the song of a bird on a hazel wand that
is distinct and characteristic of you. I would surely send a
copy to Mr Gibbings—The Orchard—Waltham Saint Lawrence—Readings—Berks—I would write a reserved and complimentary letter but I would not mention my name as I
think he might be more interested if he thought you were
an independent admirer! Thank you for asking about my
health—I am thankful to say I am responding in a wonderful way to the crisp dry air and can now walk and visit the
houses of the peasants which is a great pleasure to me—I
have been sad because my old doctor [Dr. Frey] who attended me 25 years ago died suddenly. I was lucky to have
seen him again and his prognosis of my case was favourable
and he gave me good cheer. The peasants in the valley are
bold and independent—What vulgarity there is may be at-
tributed to the English visitors who make the Hotel ring
with their gramophones and pretentious noisy voices! I do
hope you will soon have a good job again. The word job
is derived from the Mediaeval word iob a lump—to work by
the iob or lump, perhaps of Celtic origin—Good luck to you.
                         Yours sincerely
                         Llewelyn Powys
[vertically in the margin]

It was very courteous of you to send ~~Alyse~~ [the given name
is canceled] Miss Gregory a volume also. She was very
pleased.

LP-26: LLEWELYN POWYS TO KENNETH HOPKINS

                         [Postcard:
                         Clavadel,
                         February 15, 1937]
Valentine's Day
    Thank you for your letter. I am glad your poems sold so
well. I am still getting better I am glad to say[1]—Do not

---

[1] The compliment seems mixed, but Powys several times used
scrannel in this sense of thin and light, rather than the harsher
meaning given it by Milton—and by Lamb, in describing the grating
Easter anthems at Christ's Hospital.

---

[1] But two letters written three days apart during this same week—to

neglect any intellectual interest—Continue to apply yourself with the passionate intensity of a monk—The art of
life consists in breaking through the shell of one's destined
environment and learning to be at ease above and below
and to the East and West.

Yours
L. P.

LP-27: LLEWELYN POWYS TO KENNETH HOPKINS

Clavadel
Davos Platz
March 12, 1937

Dear Kenneth Hopkins,

Thank you for your letter. I am very glad to hear that
you have got this new work[1]—I think it will suit you better
than your former work and I hope you will be able to make
a success of it. We both thought it very kind of you to offer
to decorate our little bedroom but you must not think any
more of this generous plan for we may be staying another
year and more out here and our future in any case is too
undecided for us to wish to take advantage of your most
kind offer.

My health is steadily improving and I hope very much
this will continue.

I very much hope my "Twelve Months" will be published in early summer. I have been told by Mr Unwin that

---

Phyllis Playter and Bernard Taylor—gave less hopeful details: "I
cannot manage Lisaly's rich diet and that is a fact. . . . It is my
eating that is the trouble now." "My chest continues to improve
but I have had to keep in bed three days and never again will I
leave my frugal diet."

[1] Hopkins' journal entry on March 16 is laconic: "I have been employed about a month by William Burgess, Ltd. as a traveller." The
firm sold building materials; Hopkins traveled to the villages within
thirty miles of Bournemouth, and admits having covered more
thoroughly those villages that had a bookshop. Of the decorating
suggestion he has recently said that he probably offered to supply
the paint and wallpaper, but not to apply them.

this is the intention of the new firm.[2] In early April a 3 guinea "Book of Days" with a quotation from my work for every day of the year collected by John Wallis is to be published by the Cockerel Press. Also another special edition is to appear of extracts from letters written to me by a poet Miss May Chesshire[3] with an introduction by J. C. P. This is published by a man named Stuart Guthrie—but he has now gone out of business—but if you wrote to him c/o Dr John Johnson—The University Printing Press Oxford—you could get information—but it would not be worth your while to buy even if you could afford the £1..10..0. "Rats in the Sacristy" came back to me here because I thought I might have it published by Watts but I have now sent it back to America as Mr Van Wyck Brooks thought he could place it at Scribners—I hope to have my Somerset Essays ready for the autumn—Now I have told you all. I hear that the Penguin Edition are proposing to republish Ebony and Ivory.

Good luck to you in your new venture.

Yours sincerely
Llewelyn Powys

[Vertically in the margin of page one]

Thank you for letting me see your poem—"A Captive Freed." It has spirit and I like it—but you have yet to find your perfect expression.

---

[2] The Bodley Head, reorganized after bankruptcy.

[3] Miss Chesshire was ill and Llewelyn had sent her books and encouraged her in her recovery. The single published letter *from* Powys to Miss Chesshire includes this: ". . . you have concluded that I am not married to Miss Gregory. This was natural enough as she likes to keep her own name, but we were formally married by my cousin Father Johnson, a Cowley Father, at Kingston, New York [1924], with J. C. P. and Richard leGallienne as our witnesses, so you see your most exacting demands have been scrupulously put into practise." Stuart Guthrie, who had founded Cock Robin Press, died during World War II. His father was James Guthrie of the Peartree Press.

LP-28: LLEWELYN POWYS TO KENNETH HOPKINS

Clavadel
Davos Platz
Switzerland
March 31, 1937

Dear Kenneth Hopkins,

I must thank you for your letter. I am very glad that you like your new work—If you excel in it you will find a livelihood I think much more to your taste—I was glad to hear your news. I was very happy to have the little volume of Matthew Arnold and I *had* regretted having left my volume behind—but what an awful photograph of the poet at the beginning—how is it possible for so great and wise a man to look so smug? It was a graceful thought to send me the little book and I value it very much.

There is no sign yet of the snow melting up here—but indications of the spring are plentiful—The air is so clear and the edges of the mountains seem to cut so sharply against the cerulean sky that it is like living in some planetary region that has more to do with the stars and the sun than the cities of men. It was stupid of me not to have come here at once.

It is wonderful to look out at midnight onto luminous levels of lunar light far above the timber-line—snow fields so far away and yet so clearly visible. I am afraid I cannot give you the little proof that so pleases you as it would break the set—Mr Gibbings[1] gave me especially, one of each, writing his name and my name upon them, but when I get home I will look for something to take its place. I am very glad to hear you have Montaigne—I beg you to read him with great concentration—Do not allow your collecting interests[2] to carry you too far—I would like you to be first

---

[1] Robert Gibbing's engravings for The Bodley Head limited edition (one hundred copies) of *Twelve Months*. Gibbings later gave Hopkins a signed proof of the engraving for June in *Twelve Months*.

[2] The missing letters from Hopkins to Powys undoubtedly had news of his growing library. His journal for March 26 lists purchases

a poet and afterwards a collector of wisdom. I am glad Mr Venn is a little better. *Do not waste a moment of your time—* Bless you

Yours sincerely
Llewelyn Powys

[On the flap of the envelope, in Llewelyn Powys' hand]

Surely the books would be safe if sent here.

LP-29: LLEWELYN POWYS TO KENNETH HOPKINS

Clavadel
Davos Platz
April [7, 1937]

Dear Kenneth Hopkins,

I think if you write a letter to Mr Gibbings asking whether he would be willing to sign your copy of Twelve Months no harm would be done. Thank you for letting me see the two poems. The longer one is I think the better of the two though the short one has its appeal also.

I have always been attracted by the Rising Sun.[1] It was a good idea to stay there. I hope you will not desert the cliffs of White Nose for London town

> Beware the painted prostitutes' Abode
> Shun the lewd precincts of the Edgware Road!

The snow is still deep on the roads and the spring approach is tardy—There is the sound of running water "not so very far under ground" and the calling of the Yaffle and in these sounds we have cheer.

Yours sincerely
Llewelyn Powys

---

ranging from Percy Lubbock and "Solomon Eagle" (J. C. Squire was a Cambridge contemporary of Llewelyn's) to Middleton and Montaigne (the five-volume edition, described in a later letter, cost him £1). It was probably a remark similar to this diary note—at the foot of a list of new acquisitions—that provoked Llewelyn's caution about collecting: "Today I have this number of books: 740."
[1] Paul French and Kenneth Hopkins stayed at The Rising Sun Inn at East Knighton during a trip at Easter.

KH-13: KENNETH HOPKINS TO LLEWELYN POWYS

125, Southcote Road
Bournemouth.
May 17, 1937

Dear Mr. Powys,

I have had quite an exciting time recently, one way and another.

Yesterday I had tea with Mr. Gibbings at his home; it was a great privilege to meet him, and he was very kind and made me welcome. I slept Saturday night at "The Horse & Crown," about 1½ miles from Waltham S. Lawrence. In the morning I went into London to look at the decorated streets[1] and shops—some of the decorations are magnificent. Then, returning, I made my visit to Mr. Gibbings. He shewed me his work, the great stone figure of a woman he is carving, the blocks for engravings in a new book, drawings, books—everything. And what a charming companion he is! It was a wonderful time for me. Yesterday evening I slept at Odiham, and today on my way home I have visited Selborne, the home of Gilbert White the Naturalist.

But I am tired!—for I have ridden nearly 200 miles in the week-end. I bought a very early novel of Louis Marlow's —"The Puppet's Dallying" 1905, a good copy, too. If you care to borrow it when you return I shall be happy to send it along—perhaps you have not read it; it has certain immaturities of style, but I like it. I recently acquired his "Swan's Milk."

Do you remember how your brother tells in his Autobiography of his London street-girl friend, Lily? Perhaps you knew her yourself? Well! By something which seems a miracle, I have actually acquired the copy of Mr. de Kantzow's "Ultima Verba" which J. C. P. gave to Lily! It is inscribed "Lily from Jack—June 1903," and before you read this will be once again in your brother's hands, after 34 years of adventure and separation and who knows where Lily is, or

---

[1] The Coronation of George VI was on May 12, 1937.

how she came to part with this book, which I found in Bournemouth![1]

I have a lovely white-buckram bound Montaigne in 5 vols—published originally at £6..6..0, a superb edition which I bought quite cheaply in new condition. Also recently I secured a very fine edition in 2 vols. of Villon.

I send with this two new poems and a little picture of Thomas Hardy to remind you of home.[2] The country is lovely now, and bluebells fill all the Dorset woods.

I hope to hear that you are still improving in health and that Miss Gregory is well. Mr. J. C. P. tells me he will be at Chaldon in July, and Mr. Gibbings is off to Bermuda in June—lucky chap!

Yours sincerely
Kenneth Hopkins

[Vertically in the margin, opposite "I had tea with Mr. Gibbings."]

By appointment of course.

---

[1] Hopkins' discovery of the prostitute's presentation copy set off a round of letters among J. C. P., Louis Wilkinson, Hopkins, and others that is a short story—humorous and nostalgic—in itself.

[2] Hardy's name was not certain to bring only happy memories. Thomas Hardy is one of Powys' *Thirteen Worthies*—the last worthy in the book—but in 1920, just home from Africa, Llewelyn told John of a visit to the eighty-year-old Wessexman:

> I went to see Thomas Hardy one day, I had an idea that I would get inspiration from him. What do I find?—a very old dapper country sparrow of Tom Tit, unaware that I had ever seen him before or was in any way connected with literature.

But the letter was from those despondent months when Llewelyn, having published but one-third of a book, could also say to John, "Five years in Africa produces a tiny sketch and then I find I am written out."

Later there was some awkwardness about T. F.'s comment about Hardy quoted in *Skin for Skin*—a remark which Llewelyn deleted two years later from the English edition of 1927, more because of T. F.'s wishes, it would seem, than Florence Hardy's—who soon forgave them both. (I find no record of Hardy's reaction.)

"Hardy," said Theodore, "never attacks God to His face. All his sly sallies are directed at His back, but perhaps it is only this part that God has ever presented to him."

LP-31: LLEWELYN POWYS TO KENNETH HOPKINS

[Clavadel
June 20, 1937][1]

My dear Kenneth Hopkins,
Thank you for the photograph of Robert Gibbings—It is an interesting picture but I have seen better ones of him. The coin is a great pleasure for me to possess—I value it very much. I like to hear of your successes in the bookshops —I think you were lucky to come upon the Confessions of Two Brothers—which is now very scarce.
Of the poems I like the poem to Jean better than the one to Anne[2]—but I think both are good *in their vein*. It was good of you to let me see them. I am very delighted with Switzerland—largely I suppose because the country has given me back my health—I think I shall often come back here. I like the mountains and the people and the cattle and the deer, and the marmots and the field mice—which are as large as our water rats—The whole country now is res-onant with the sound of the cattle bells and the sound of running water.

Yours sincerely
Llewelyn Powys

---

[1] The Bodley Head *Advice to a Young Poet* dates this letter (**XXIX**) "July 20th, 1937," but the postmark is clearly "20.VI.37"; and Hopkins' diary entry of June 25, 1937, says, "Llewelyn writes that he intends returning often to Switzerland."
[2] The several poems to Anne—and to Ann—make positive identifica-tion impossible, but one illustrates a farther use of a manuscript book—by a poet whose journal often shows gaps of three and four months. The sestet of the seventh sonnet (in a sequence of twenty-eight) starts:

O Ann, I know your will is to ensnare,
You do not feel as those who love you feel
You're proud, uncaring, chaste beyond compare,
In you lies beauty trapped and safely sealed.

In pencil, a footnote in Hopkins' hand reads: "1941—not now I bet. Didn't I see her in Edgware Road?" And still later, in ink: "1942— Indeed I did, and once in Bryanston Square."

LP-32: LLEWELYN POWYS TO KENNETH HOPKINS

Clavadel
Davos Platz
Switzerland
August 2, 1937

Dear Kenneth Hopkins

Thank you for your interesting letter and for your sonnets which I liked very much. I am answering at once because I wish to get the photograph of your pretty Lady safe back into your hands. I am happy that you have had so enjoyable a Coronation summer.

The weather here has been a little doubtful but we have enjoyed many good walks in the woods and even sometimes above the timber line where the lawns are very fresh and near the sky. It is in many ways an attractive country—The peasant houses on the Alps are always full of interest for me, these old old houses that are only used in the summer months. They are roofed with shingles which because of the rain and snow acquire a silvery look—like the back of a silver scaled fish whereas the log walls get coloured by the sun to the darkest russet; and it is so hot because of the rarefied nature of the atmosphere that the moss with which they line or pad the inter spaces between the logs often appears black where it has been charred by the burning heat. In the very early morning I like to see the shadow of one mountain fall across another. You must remember my warning about not being too exacting of my brother's time. He is very defenceless and you must not be taken in by his civil manners—I would not wish him to be troubled through an introduction of mine and do not forget that personal diffidence is in itself a grace.

Good luck.

Yours sincerely
Llewelyn Powys

[Vertically in the margin of page one]

I will be very happy to inscribe your copy of the Confessions if you send it to me here.

Kenneth Hopkins' friendship with John Cowper Powys was progressing famously. The warmth of his letters to Hopkins transcended all civility; and on a visit to Chaldon Herring where John was vacationing from July 24 to 26, 1937, Kenneth saw more of the eldest brother than he ever had of Llewelyn. After returning to Merionethshire John wrote, on August 12:

> I like to think of the way—like Brother Llewelyn—you *dig in* to your native soil for your Prestige as a poet as well as your happiness as a Wanderer. I recall Hardy saying 40 odd years ago just that very thing that he preferred a quiet half glory *"in situ"* to all the acclamation of the Duchesses in London Town!

And two weeks later he told Hopkins, "You [and Llewelyn] are of the same *School of the Sun* and needn't incur or undergo all the recondite self-questionings of the votaries of the Moon!"

This second letter is in answer to Hopkins' query of how—and whether—to ask Llewelyn for a foreword to a new volume, *Poems and Sonnets*, which he was preparing to submit to publishers. John showed often that he was aware of his brother's efforts to shield him from the encroaching world, and may even have enjoyed the irony of counseling a potential intruder on how to approach Llewelyn. John wrote to Kenneth:

> I would boldly write to Llewlyn and ask for his Foreword— because in your and his case—with so much downright ways between ye I don't think there need be the least salty grain of the awkwardness you speak of—even if he *did* bluntly and roundly refuse! No harm would have been done to either of you if he did—He would have his own reasons and whatever they were they needn't discourage you; and *wouldn't;* nor is *he* one to experience that kind of uneasy remorse that *some* would at a refusal—whereas if he agreed—all would be well. So my advice would be

to go ahead—*Take it lightly:* and be ready to take a refusal lightly and not be fussed in either way. . . .

Second Question:
Yes *certainly* send his Foreword along with the MS to the Publishers—or to the Literary Agent if you decide on using one. . . . My own agent is a good one. His name is *Laurence Pollinger* Esq.

Third Question:
No: I have never heard of offering (or paying) any fee for such a Foreword. I don't think *that* is ever done.[1]

LP-33: LLEWELYN POWYS TO KENNETH HOPKINS

[Clavadel
September 4, 1937]

Dear Mr Hopkins
   I write in haste. When you have got your poems in order I would be very happy to read them through—I do not think you have really reached a position when it would be wise to publish—I think you should allow your powers to mature. In my opinions your poetry is still too derivative and does not express with truth the intensity of your nature. However, if your heart is set upon publishing I will read your book and if you still wish write a few words to serve as a Preface but you must not expect me to say more than I feel— I do not think you have yet found a natural expression in your poetry for your emotional experience—You often nearly do and then some line reminds the reader of the poet's artistry.
   My advice to you is to wait—a little—Do not waste a moment—Live, live, live—and then little by little your nature will find its own deep and harmonious expression.
                                        Yours sincerely
                                        Llewelyn Powys

_____

[1] But see Llewelyn's offer to Theodore Dreiser, reported in *Verdict of Bridlegoose* (London, 1927) pp. 41–42.

LP-34: LLEWELYN POWYS TO KENNETH HOPKINS

[Clavadel
September 14, 1937]

Dear Kenneth Hopkins
    I enclose the Preface—I hope it will answer your purpose. Good luck to you—You have I think an authentic poetic gift but it is still undeveloped and its cadence now here now there—now come[1] and now gone.
                        Yours sincerely
                        Llewelyn Powys
                        Sept 12th 1937

PREFACE

Mr Kenneth Hopkins is a native of Bournemouth, a watering place that to many of us who live to the west of Poole Harbour seems a veritable fortress of unpoetical prosperity, and it is encouraging to know that such a citadel of modernity is capable of producing so wayward a child of Parnassus. "Where you least look for it there starts the hare."[2]
The most important poetry of the human race has been concerned either with nature, war, or love. Mr Kenneth Hopkins' subject is love and these verses will have an especial appeal to all lovers whether they be sad or happy. In a beautiful poem Matthew Arnold has expressed the longing that all true lovers experience to stay the passing of time:

> With sweet join'd voices
> And with eyes brimming
> "Ah", they cry, "Destiny,
> Prolong the present!
> Time! Stand still here!"[3]

---

[1] Llewelyn Powys wrote, "now gone and now gone." This emendation—made at Alyse Gregory's suggestion—is the sole change I have made in transcribing from the original letters. Compare Llewelyn's judgment with John Cowper Powys' comment—"too quick come and too quick gone"—on page 126, above.

[2] Sancho Panza.

[3] "Consolation," x.

Mr Hopkins' verses contain recurring meditations upon the transitory nature of our existence here in earth and their sadder tones come as wistfully to the ear as the notes of a blackbird's song from a twilight hedge in April.

> And over seas and over hills, I know
> And over forest trees and lovely lakes
> Swift passionate flights of birds for ever go.

His poem to the White Nose—the noblest of all the Dorset headlands—will give pleasure to many people who have enjoyed hours of summer freedom on that wild cliff.

> All behind us silence, moving clouds, the hills,
> Summer twilight deepening,
> And our time of love.[4]

Llewelyn Powys
September 1937

Hopkins' *Poems and Sonnets* was rejected by Cobden-Sanderson and Penguin, and not until 1944 was his first hard-cover volume of poetry, *Love and Elizabeth*, published (without a preface) by Sylvan Press, under the editorial aegis of Charles Williams. But he continued to write: a terse diary entry for September notes the receipt

---

[4] From the first poem in Hopkins' *Collected Poems: 1935–1965*—although the poems are not arranged in order of composition:

White Nose, Dorset

> Where the hills are
> And the sea below
> And the shadowy island in the bay
>
> We have found
> Certain homes for loving, you and I
> Watching stadowy island and the sea below.
>
> All behind us silence, moving clouds, the hills,
> Summer twilight deepening
> And our time of love.
>
> Silent shadowy island
> Lovers on the hill
> And the sea, below.

of Llewelyn's Preface—the regrets he knows he will have about not keeping "a careful record of every day as John Cowper suggested"—and the purchase of "a typewriter so that now I send almost daily poems to magazines—unsuccessfully." And two new poems went off to Switzerland, where Llewelyn was pressing forward to complete *Love and Death,* abandoned at the time of his severe hemorrhages in 1933. The first poem foreshadows the biography Kenneth was to start writing the following year:

To His Mistress Reading A Spelling Book

I play on you as somewhere I have heard
John Donne was apt to play upon a word,
Weave meaning in and out as I in you
And you in me are sometimes wont to do;
I wonder if from word-play master Donne
Had half as much or half as worthy fun?

She Maketh This Reply:

If Donne loved words, as somewhere you have heard,
So much that he performed upon a word
In, out, out, in, his meaning seems to me
Not more intricate than when lovingly
You upon me those curious courses run
As skillfully as ever did John Donne.

LP-35: LLEWELYN POWYS TO KENNETH HOPKINS

[Clavadel]
October 11, 1937

Dear Kenneth Hopkins,
    Thank you for your letter and for the poems. I liked the one entitled To His Mistress Reading a Spellingbook the best. This has charming play in it—though the word "fun" strikes me as not quite up to the level of the poem. I like also "Hold me more close etc."
    It interests me to know you like the autumn and winter better than the summer—I cannot share your feeling—I love

sunshine too much. Yes I am very sorry for poor Mrs Venn—
and I shall miss Mr Venn when I get back to England.

We are having some rather dismal weather here—but I
hope as the season advances it will get better.

Yours sincerely
Llewelyn Powys

AG-7: ALYSE GREGORY TO KENNETH HOPKINS

Clavadel
Davos Platz,
Switzerland.
December 10, 1937

Dear Mr. Hopkins,

I am sorry to have to write you that Mr. Powys has had
another severe hemorrhage of the lungs and is still very ill.
He was able to read your letter, however—or rather he asked
me to read it to him—and he was pleased by the little book
you sent him of Donne's love poems. I hope he will have
recovered from this attack sufficiently in a month's time for
us to feel free of anxiety—but he who lives on hope treads
on cobwebs. The snow is very beautiful here and the birds
come to our balcony for seeds—and the children go by on
skis.

Your ardor is wonderful—and I hope it will be rewarded—
but what are rewards? As my brother-in-law writes—"we
should be crafty, obstinate, and lonely."

Sincerely yours,
Alyse Gregory

AG-8: ALYSE GREGORY TO KENNETH HOPKINS

Clavadel,
Davos Platz,
Switzerland.
December 27, 1937

Dear Mr. Hopkins,

Your little books fell into our snowy mountains like
blossoms from a very different climate. Mr. Wilkinson is
here too and has either written you or intends to. My
husband is still too ill either to read or to write.

You are both young and a poet and attentive to the raging beat of your own heart, and I do not know whether Matthew Arnold is right when he says that poetry is nine tenths energy and one tenth imagination, but I am sure you have both energy and imagination. And I so hope you are rewarded in the ensuing year by having a book of your poems published. We are both touched and charmed by these collections.

Sincerely yours,
Alyse Gregory

John Cowper Powys had introduced Kenneth Hopkins to Louis Wilkinson by letter, earlier that month, and Wilkinson was soon as regular a writer of letters to Bournemouth as the two Powyses; by the time of Llewelyn's death, Kenneth's total of numbered letters—envelopes, rather, for he saved them—was: John—62; Llewelyn—48; Louis—39. The letter of introduction, dated December 11, 1937, appears in John Cowper's *Letters to Louis Wilkinson*:

> Just a line, my dear—and don't be cross—but a young lad aged 23 exactly, called Kenneth Hopkins, whose address is 125 Southcote Road, Bournemouth, Hants, is a very very great admirer (and collector too) of your works—and is longing to get into epistolary touch with your Retired Leisure. "He is a great hand," as my Father would say, at amorous and indeed lecherous poetry—but he also has two unpublished volumes of more orthodox verse (which Lulu and I like well), one with an introduction by Lulu and one (privately printed already) with one by me. When he was a still younger lad he attended your lectures in Bournemouth and wrote essays for you[1] . . . but he can't wait for the slow revolving prospect of your return as a speaker—and he swears on his heart that he won't be a bother or a nuisance to you.

---

[1] In 1930 or 1931—two or three years after he had left school at age fourteen—Kenneth attended six lectures by Louis Wilkinson sponsored by University Extension Lectures. The essays he wrote, and Wilkinson criticized, are not now available.

I have found him a *most* easy and entertaining lad—with a lot of tact—and by no means a fool—and he is nice-looking and a terrific bibliophile.

Phyllis likes him as much as I do; we've seen him several times now. . . . I thought best to write and send *his* address to *you* rather than your address to *him*.

But the existence of what he calls a "bawdy" poem—but really it's not a bawdy poem but an eager youthful poetical lecherous poem—called "The Progress of Love" would be enough of a colourable reason for your addressing him a note with your London address and asking him for further particulars of this poem, "so spoken of by my friend Mr. John Powys."

Don't 'ee be cross, honey, and no need to bother to reply *here* if you consent to drop a line *there*.

yr. J.

I haven't yet had a *really* reassuring letter from Clavadel about Lulu's picking up after this curst new haemorrhage out there.

LP-36: LLEWELYN POWYS TO KENNETH HOPKINS

[Postcard:
Clavadel,
February 10, 1938]

Dear Mr Kenneth Hopkins—

I was interested to hear of all you had done and especially of your climb down the landslide at White Nose. You must not ask for or expect any literary criticism or appreciation till my health improves—I am glad all goes well with you. Continue to read and write and live day and night but always with understanding.

Yours sincerely
Llewelyn Powys

LP-37: LLEWELYN POWYS TO KENNETH HOPKINS

Chydyok[1]
Chaldon Herring
Dorchester, Dorset
England
March 18, 1938

Dear Kenneth Hopkins,

I am very sorry indeed to hear that you have had this difficulty—My own advice to you would be to try to get work in some book shop, preferably second hand or on the staff of a newspaper. I do not feel as if you will ever do much in the commercial world. Where the treasure is there will be the heart also—and I do not think, try as you may, you will ever be able to give that "yellow slave" the consideration necessary for a financial success. These money-makers are quick to smell out poets as a cat a mouse—Better live poor and content than rich and under conditions that are unsympathetic. I liked the poem you sent me. I am still far from well and am troubled by the same weakness in the eyes that tormented me at Chydyok but I thought I would like to send you a word—and my sincere hope that you once more fall on your feet. You should try to discover exactly why they thought you lacking—go below their civility—and get the truth—the actual truth however unpleasing. In the meantime—remember that life is more important than any success and to be aware of the rising and setting of the sun of more value than great wealth. Go to the libraries—Read, think, talk—Learn good manners—and honesty of the mind— Learn to speak well and shake hands with an honest grip and not limp as a dead fish—be much by yourself—by the seashore, at night—by rivers and streams and lakes—squint at the moon and worship the sun.

Yours sincerely
Llewelyn Powys

---

[1] The use of his old address—fifteen months after leaving that home—seems quite a slip, even by an ill man, but Alyse Gregory, in the Introduction to his *Letters,* wrote of his irresponsible and inaccurate mind about small details: he spelled "to the end of his days the names of two members of his family and one of his closest friends incorrectly, and constantly misdirect[ed] letters."

Kenneth Hopkins' diary reference to this most recent loss of job is terser than the others. In its entirety, this is his entry for March 19, 1937—the day after Llewelyn responded from Switzerland:

> Wilkinson and I get on very well by letter and exchange views of the art of love. I am again temporarily unemployed. War seems not far off but will probably not come. My recent sonnet, "The loom of age winds our young summer in" was hailed by John Cowper as the best Shakespearean sonnet not by S he'd ever seen.
>
> Recent purchases, almost nil, but a very fine oak bookcase among them.
>
> I have lost Muriel and for a time at least also I have lost Margaret. Doris will not lie with me and all's unwell! But things will be better, and I must trust in God![1]

There are no further entries in the journal until 1946; nor does Hopkins' autobiography offer much information about his departure from ironmongery:

> My final break with the trade of Builders' Merchant came with the termination of my engagement with Burgess's. . . . In the early days when I used to get the sack it seemed plausible to blame my employers. They were, after all, but fallible men, more expert perhaps in putty and glass than in recognising exceptional possibilities in poetical apprentices. And I did keep my first job over four years.
>
> But here and there it was now beginning to be thought that there might be faults on both sides. And there was another difficulty: Bournemouth did not furnish a limitless supply of Builders' Merchants. I had already been released from the pay-rolls of four of them. . . . [his ellipsis] The remaining three entered into no strong competition for my services.
>
> I thought the time had come for me to be a writer. . . .

In 1965 Kenneth Hopkins suggested that his practicing of ironic submission—following Llewelyn's advice after

---

[1] At the end of this line, with a darker pencil: " (!)"

an earlier dismissal—was, perhaps, audible.[2] On the final morning at William Burgess Ltd., the Head Traveller (to-day's title would be Sales Manager) said "Good morning," and got back from Hopkins, "And good morning to you." Given this line, a novice actor would find little to get his teeth into, but a man who has scripted Utterpug and stood in as Felicia the Winsome—on short notice— needs not great lines.

As Hopkins picked up his terminal pay, his determination hardened.

> Rather than hang about out of work in Bournemouth I would be a tramp! I would shuffle along the lanes and support myself by selling my poems from door to door! My parents heard this declaration with proper scepticism and decided that the way to cure such foolishness was to acquiesce. All right, be a tramp then!

The Corruption of a Poet goes on with the details of disengagement, a matter of a fortnight:

> I began to settle up my large affairs. I sold a good many of my books, retaining only so many as would go in the large glass-fronted bookcase that had been one of my twenty-first birthday presents. My mother paid my tailor's bill. I distributed various personal effects here and there: most of my maps to Paul, my Primus stove on long loan to Bob. . . . I presented—very grandly—a set of the works of Edgar Allan Poe to the library, and—very foolishly—a set of the *Biographia Britannica*. . . .
>
> I cannot exactly recall what equipment I took for this adventure but my mother, mildly sarcastic, pointed out that tramps could hardly be permitted sheets and pillows. I took one blanket and a groundsheet to serve until I got accustomed to sleeping under old newspapers, and a rucksack. . . . The night before I left, Shindy and I went round sev-

---

[2] Hopkins is also my source for an irrelevant fact. There was until not too long ago a punishable crime of silence in the British Army called "dumb insolence."

eral pubs and talked with increasing wisdom as the hours
passed, of the things we had known. Shindy, I think, thought
of me as one already dead. The rest of my acquaintances
expected me home again with a cold in the head by the
end of the week.

Corwen, Merionethshire, North Wales, was to be an
early and brief stopping point before the real destination,
London, and on the day before departure Hopkins wrote
to John Cowper Powys Esq. at that address:

7 April 28

    This is my last bit of typing! for an hour hence I shall
have pawned my machine! . . .
    All's prepared, packed, sealed, and ready! save for one
dolorous blow—I can't find my great good noble king hat
of them all! So I have taken an oath to go hatless. . . .
    Now I will enclose two sonnets more to shew that I've not
been idle, and I'll away to confer with my pawnshop keeper.
    Words further of my dealings with the world and of my
deeds and of my journey's progress and of all the things
I do will reach you in due course; so, FAREWELL!

Kenneth

P.S. I feel like an anchor that's dragged from its darling
mud, or a tooth most rudely plucked from age old roots—
for all my life now is behind me and another life begins;
being new-born is odd, but pleasant!

[Vertically, in pencil, in the margin]

P.S. If you want to write about anything, c/o W. Dibben . . .
Bristol will reach me up to Monday morning first post—after
that my address is K. H.

THE WORLD!

But 125 Southcote Road, Bournemouth, was still the de-
livery point (the postcard shows no forwarding address)
for a note, dated April 6, from Davos Platz:

LP-38: LLEWELYN POWYS TO KENNETH HOPKINS

[Postcard:
Clavadel,
April 6, 1938]

Thank you for your six sonnets. I like them all but especially perhaps the first. Good luck to you on your historic pilgrimage! May the strong influence of the sun and sweet influence of the moon and magical influence of the stars be ever with you—and the stiles you leap over be easy and all the footpath ways you follow lucky—Take a note book with you, see, hear, smell, taste, feel and record all—Avoid the main streets. Keep to the alleys—and the open.

Yours sincerely
Llewelyn Powys

8

Letters: Davos Platz and London
June 12, 1938, to August 28, 1939

LP-39: LLEWELYN POWYS TO KENNETH HOPKINS[1]

Clavadel
Davos Platz
Switzerland
June 12, 1938

Dear Kenneth Hopkins,

Thank you for your interesting letter and for the poem which I liked. I had heard news of you from Mr Wilkinson— I think you are doing very wisely to make the best of this time and I would aim at getting attached to some publishing house. In the meantime work on your book at the Museum and Look and Live. Of course I would have no objection to your undertaking the bibliography—I think one has been made up by a gentleman of Cincinnati, Lloyd Emerson Siberell but I have mislaid his address—I know I sent him certain information but whether it was ever published I dont know.[2] I conclude not or I would have had a copy. In any case if the address turns up I would get in touch with him for he might be a help to you. I think the idea of the Donne book is very good—though difficult to place—Multiply your interests in every direction and leave no alley unexplored—It is good to be lonely—It is how thoughts grow

---

[1] This and all subsequent letters are addressed to Hopkins at 69 Red Lion Street, London W.C.1.
[2] It was not, although the next year Siberell wrote an introduction for the American edition of *Baker's Dozen*.

and ideas that "have hands and feet." I send you half a guinea and my blessing.

Yours sincerely
Llewelyn Powys

[Vertically in the margin]

This review in the Cincinnati Star Times was sent to me yesterday from Mr Siberell and a letter sent to the paper should find him if you think he might be of help to you.

[On the flap side of the envelope]

Please give my very especial compliments to Mr Lahr—for whom "Now the Gods are Dead" was originally written.[3]

The half guinea from Davos Platz was welcome. After hitchhiking north from Bournemouth and spending several days in Corwen, Wales, Kenneth Hopkins arrived in London on Maundy Thursday "with two and eightpence ha'-penny"—less than forty cents today—but, according to a budget he kept in the fall of 1938, Kenneth paid 1-3/4d. for a half pint of milk (twopence when he did not bring a container), 3d. for cheese, 1-1/2d. for dripping (quantities not given), 5d. for beer ("a pint of mild"), and five shillings a week for a room over Charles Lahr's bookshop on Red Lion Street.

Mere extracts from Hopkins' autobiography tend to strip away amplitude of heart and humor, leaving only pence and impertinence, but the lighthearted telling is there—and the facts are accurate:

---

[3] In the 1920's Lahr and his wife, E. Archer, at the Blue Moon Press, published D. H. Lawrence's *Pansies*, several of T. F. Powys' shorter works, and others. But *Now that the Gods are Dead* was never printed in England until the Bodley Head edition in 1949. In June, 1965, Alyse Gregory said, "It was *Glory of Life* Llewelyn wrote at the instigation of Mr. Lahr. *Now that the Gods are Dead* was written at the request of Lynd Ward."

A fair sprinkling of the customers (a courtesy term) who used Charlie's shop as a club were either on the dole or about to be and thus I had at my command the best of advice. On the Tuesday after Easter I went to sign on; and in due course I received not only a weeks' money for the current week, but arrears from the time I left Bournemouth which amounted to about thirty shillings. That fixed me up financially though I am bound to confess the whole business was very inconvenient. I had to report for duty three times a week at the Labour Exchange off Pentonville Road—and that . . . . cost me about sixpence a week in fares to collect their miserable pittance. A bit later on, during the war, another friend of mine *had the money brought to him* (so he said) because he told the Manager seventeen shillings wasn't worth going to collect in bad weather. But my friend had a black beard, and a cultured manner, which made a difference. Once you get a half-starved look, like I had, they kick you around something dreadful. . . .

My next step was to get a ticket for the British Museum Reading Room, and this I accomplished without any difficulty, backed by the powerful name of John Cowper Powys —and was I not myself represented in the Catalogue by a Work—*Twelve Poems.*

Sporadically Hopkins had jobs—selling self-sealing wrappers to newspaper publishers, selling a reference book on the English novel, gathering voter lists, clerking in the post office during the Christmas season, and twice the Labour Exchange sent him out to employers. But these were periods of waiting for a new series of dole payments to start.

His preoccupation, as always, was writing. For some months he worked at the British Museum on a life of Donne; he wrote at a novel, *Poor Heretic* (unpublished), whose hero Christopher Adams lived at Charles Lear's bookshop on Red Lion Street; he "wrote Seven Sonnets in $1\frac{3}{4}$ hours at the B. M."; and he wrote letters. From John Cowper Powys alone, in the first five months in London, he received—and answered—seventeen letters (while getting only two from the ailing Llewelyn); and beginning in June the letters from Wales were signed "Your great uncle John."

LP-40: LLEWELYN POWYS TO KENNETH HOPKINS

Clavadel
Davos Platz
Switzerland
September 6, 1938

Dear Kenneth Hopkins

I was very happy to receive your beautiful card of Corfe Castle and to know that you were still prospering in London. You must not be disappointed about your present difficulties in selling your literary gifts—It is a good thing not to be successful too early. See all you can, hear all you can, smell all you can, taste all you can, and feel all you can. Live healthy like a good countryman—up early to walk by the river—explore May Fair *and* Wapping Old Stairs—talk to all on benches and at coffee stalls—Go to Covent Garden at 3am as Oscar Wilde used to do to watch the market carts bring in their waggon loads of produce "like green jade" and stand to admire the rainbow sheen that covers the ribs of the pigeons. I regard this time in your life as very important, better, far better than going to Oxford and Cambridge—but you must not waste a moment—nor be content to live as other men—

You must live as one under orders but not under orders to make money or be successful—but under orders to be happy, to understand, to Live. Wash your body at the Red Lion conduit and your bucks in the Thames if need be—be always spotlessly clean and live on herbs and bread and water. Never miss looking up at the sun with cognizance—watching the river flow by—observing how the world wags in bawdy houses—taking the holy sacrament today and tomorrow watching the coots in the rushes of Hyde Park—have eyes for all—and never be content with the second rate. Visit museums and libraries—let your mind fly free and let no labour for it be too exacting if you are likely to gain sensibility and understanding—Take notes, observe—write always —Live like a starling picking up where you can—like a kid

on Mount Ida—and more serious than a raven in February
nesting on Swyre Head or White Nose—

Compel your mind to break through the commonplace—
free yourself from the importunate pressures of each day
and keep a shrike's eye always open when you eat and when
you make love and when you look out of your window at
night—Watch your health carefully, live with license but
with *strictest* control also—Remember young men *may* die
while old men must.

Yours,
Llewelyn Powys

[Vertically in the margin of page one]

Please remember me very kindly to Mr Lahr—I hope to
meet him again one day.

Kenneth Hopkins' letters to John Cowper Powys and
Louis Wilkinson (at those times when Wilkinson was
away from his London flat near Kensington Gardens)
abound in details of his activities—details which must
have been, in part, set forth in the lost letters to Davos
Platz. Two letters to Wilkinson, in July and September,
1938, give the range of his doings:

My short stories [are] passed on to Curtis Brown [the agent]
to sell for me—if he can!—but the fact that Brown has not
rejected them with blows and oaths is encouraging.

My poems have been rejected with much vigour by The
Cresset Press and now lie with The Fortune Press. . . . Duck-
worth have lost interest in my Donne book. I have not lost
interest, but temporarily it is suspended. When you are here
I hope you will advise me, having seen the completed portion—I think my way of writing it is wrong—i.e. commer-
cially; my prose style is rather odd and perhaps unsuited to
the job. Poems are rare with me these days. But when we
meet I shall have a few to show you. . . .

I have forgotten my criticism of your Chaste Man [a novel
by Louis Marlow published in 1917]—which I wrote, you
remember, entirely on impulse, so it was probably hasty and
unreasoned—I cannot now therefore usefully comment

again. It was interesting to hear that Somerset Maugham
had also been talking of the book—I wonder if you shewed
him any of my poems—alas!—there I go!—as if you had
nothing else in the world to think about but my affairs!
All young men are egotistical, but by God I give points in
that to them all! . . .
    I have a superb wench, Betty the railway girl, for whom
all my other ladies may go hang, so sweet she is!—You must
meet her, so let me know when I can introduce her to you.

Hopkins has told of meeting his future wife on his first,
one-day excursion-rate trip home to Bournemouth in May.
She had been on the train in the morning, and that evening going back to London—loath to speak to a strange
girl on the Southern Railway—he wrote "May I see you
home?" on the inside cover of the book he was reading,
and passed it to her. She handed back *Rats in the Sacristy*
without making any specific promise; but when they
reached Waterloo Station it was raining. To Louis Wilkinson, half a year later, he reported that Betty Coward had
promised to marry him:

> Ho! you say, or perhaps Ha! But now I tell you that I swear
> even you with weight of years and experience greater far
> than mine, never have seen so sweet a brown wench as Betty
> is, nor one so lovable, nor one who is better fitted to bear
> the lusty sons of a poet. . . . [She is delightful] but also she
> can cook!! I like also her great skill in darning socks; these
> and like matters determine me that for one such as I with a
> healthy appetite and hard on socks into the bargain Betty is
> the wench to wed, and so I will. These things she has ap-
> proved of and sealed them with more kisses than I can
> compute. When you return you shall see and marvel, saying,
> This raw provincial poet has come to the city and carried
> off from beneath our noses the sweetest brown wench in
> London for his bride. And you will (I think) wish us well.

"Uncle John" applauded the proposal, Llewelyn did not
object, and Louis deplored the whole idea. One year later
they married.

LP-41: LLEWELYN POWYS TO KENNETH HOPKINS

Clavadel
Davos Platz
October 20, 1938

Dear Mr Kenneth Hopkins

I write in haste to thank you for your kind thought in sending this little Sentimental Journey—though as you suspected its print is too small for my eyes. I was interested to see your new sonnet which I liked well—I was very pleased to know that you have not been betrayed into taking life lightly by your new friends—It has rich gold to give for poets like you if they have sufficient resolution and passion but it is fairy gold!

I was interested by hearing of the various people you have been seeing, especially of your alliance with Miss Boine Granger[1] who is so brave a woman and so good and gifted a woman. Mr. ——[2] I have never set eyes upon. I suspect him of being exactly what I would not wish you to be. In any case he is a great boaster and great pusher of his own fortunes, and his manners are shown by the fact that he never had the civility to send me a copy of the book for which he begged a preface.

Yours sincerely
Llewelyn Powys

P.S. I am not too well and have been in bed again but I think *essentially* my condition is improving by inches.

LP-42: LLEWELYN POWYS TO KENNETH HOPKINS

[Clavadel,
December 19, 1938]

My dear Kenneth Hopkins,

Thank you for your letter and for the poems—I was happy to read them and I think you are really gifted—but I would

---

[1] Boyne Grainger, a friend of the Powyses from New York City, was visiting London.

[2] I refer to the suppression of this name in the Introduction. The next letter also mentions him.

like that your work began to show a wider vision and for
you to be able to find expression for the deeper and more
original moods that must be the harvest of your intense
personal approach to life. At present it is love alone that
gives you inspiration and Love *is* the most important thing
in the world—Love and Death—but your approach to love
remains still formal and literary. I would suggest that you
go through Hardy's poems again and see if you cannot learn
from his crooked hedge-sticks and Dorset fire-dogs how to
deepen your verse. I would like you little by little to become more understanding, more steadfast and humane—
with your vital interests more occupied with your *own* perceptions and experiences and philosophic consciousness of
existence than with your personal successes or ambitions—
For example I would not let the excitements of youth and
development dull your power of response say to your mother
and your relationship with her which you should cultivate
with all the sensibility and delicacy that is in your nature—
so that no son—no poet was ever more gentle and appreciative. Let your sympathy extend beyond the cats of the
household. I dont want you to become a kind of pushing
literary climber after the pattern of Mr. ——. "Good wares
need no chapman." If your spiritual life is not genuine and
independent and self-sufficient you will grow shallow—The
kingdom of Heaven is within you and no patronage from
others can really improve the pipkin paradise which must be
built up by you stone by stone.

Your love of London is an advance—I would wish your
interests to extend in all directions—from the light of the
starshine on the roof opposite your window to the life of the
fly in the public jakes. You must miss nothing and lose not
a moment. Have a mind easily accessible to everything that
is poetic. Edna St. Vincent Millay's address is Steepletop,
Austerlitz, New York State but I think it would be far better
to approach her in the ordinary way through her publisher
Hamish Miles in England and Harpers in America—! She
has a very large correspondence and I would prefer that you
did not make use of my name in your advances—lest she
might feel more responsible about answering your letter
than she would if you wrote as an unsponsored poet on your
own merits. I think it would be much more exciting to
arouse her interest without outside help. Emerson is now

out of fashion—but for all his provincialism he is a great
man and a simple and sincere man and a *poet* as well as a
sage. Read again his poems in the Oxford Book. It is not
fair to compare him to Voltaire—The genius of Emerson is
shown by his quick recognition of young unknown poets by
the score—the best known examples being Whitman and
James Thomson—and his protective generosity to Thoreau
was wonderful—Would you give this little keepsake to your
Betty whom I hope will please you—not only for *now*—Have
a care Prince, have a care!!!!

> Your crabbed friend and Dominie
> Llewelyn Powys

[Vertically in the right margin]

Please give my Christmas greetings to Mr and Mrs Lahr and
hopes for a lucky year for both of them.

[Vertically in the left margin]

I would not worry your head about being on the dole—get
all you can!!! You are putting the money to the best possible
use and good luck to them—only watch your health and
read about diet—and learn and live.

Kenneth Hopkins went home to Bournemouth for
Christmas week, and answered the letter from there.

KH–14: KENNETH HOPKINS TO LLEWELYN POWYS

> 125 Southcote Road
> Bournemouth
> December 29, 1938

Dear Mr Powys,
    It was kind of you to send that book to Betty, she was
delighted with it, and I value very much my little "Pictures
of Death" [Holbein's] and we both thank you.
    I have spent a quiet Christmas; I have not been to Chal-
don, unfortunately it proved impossible, but we had a happy

day at Kingston, Worth, and S Alban's Head—is it you or your brother John who speaks of "S Alban's Head" though it is really S Aldhelm's? There must be some reason for the association of S Alban with this headland, for since childhood I have heard it named so, long before I read or had heard of your books; indeed, we used to go to Swanage even when I was four or five and my mother always said S Albans.

Your last letter to me is at London, but I can remember in general your words about my poems and I want to speak of these. I won't answer the charge of being too literary, because I know it is true, though I am not sure that it is altogether a bad thing. But you say, I think, that you would like to see me relating other things than love in my poetry. I think I shall, but not for a time. As I think you know, I never write poetry unless "I feel like it," I never "make up poetry" for the sake of doing so. Consequently, I write what comes, and as long as love poetry comes I shall write it! But all the time experience is being noted and stored in my brain; sometimes I can almost feel some scene or incident being engraved in my brain, so vividly does it strike me— yet I never want to make it into a poem on the spot. When Betty leaves me at night I do not feel that our happiness must at once be recorded in a poem, yet that happiness will be recorded sooner or later in some poem, it will not be lost but is in me ready to be called upon. That is why now that I am writing almost no poetry I am not perturbed. I think when I begin working another, a new vein, of poetic ore I shall bring out brighter gold or bigger jewels than before. Periods of silence I have had before, and always the new work when it comes is an advance—or so I think.

I value your criticism and advice very greatly, I do not forget that you once said you felt like a Lord Chesterfield towards me, and that is why I have written the paragraph above. I am proud to think that you are my friend to whom I can say these things without fearing that they have no interest for you, and I want you to know that every word of your criticism is carefully read and pondered, and almost always found to be in accordance with the conclusion I have reached by following in my thought the arguement you propose.

I will send you a piece of blank verse recently written; this will shew you that I have to some extent already followed your advise—I write, in this, not of love, and I write in what for me is a novel form. The poem is only an exercise or experiment, but it is a straw to indicate that my new wind of poetry, when it arises, will blow in another direction![1]

> With every good wish for 1939!
> yours sincerely
> Kenneth Hopkins

p.s. You never say that you are well or ill; please tell me of your health.

Hopkins must have mailed the "piece of blank verse" the same day, for there was a response from Davos Platz postmarked three days later. Nothing that he sent to Llewelyn Powys had ever drawn such plaudits. The letter is heavily underscored—as rare in Llewelyn's writing as it is vitiatingly common in John Cowper Powys'. There is no indication that the eighty-eight-line poem, "The Death of Faustus," was written after Powys' advice—although Hopkins had often proved rapid in composition—but it is not farfetched to think that earlier comparisons with Marlowe had stayed with the young poet. No topic could have been more congenial to Llewelyn than the first fifty lines. After hearing the praise, Hopkins revised it somewhat and expanded it greatly—to just under 500 lines. These excerpts are from the longer version, retitled "The Moods of Faustus"; the manuscript of the unpublished poem is owned by the University of Texas:

[from] The Moods of Faustus

Argument: . . . The poem is a soliloquy, the more dramatic parts are spoken by Faustus, the more meditative parts represent his thoughts as he waits for the striking of the clock and the coming of his Master.

---

[1] The several misspellings in this letter—and Llewelyn's "whom" in the last—provoke a reminder: this transcription of the letters is literal.

     . . . This Nazarene,
Who was he?—some say, God's son, God himself,
If this oft-vaunted God indeed is three—
God then once made a bargain even as I
His creature Faustus; but my word is kept
And soon will be delivered; not so God's!
What was God's contract but a compromise?
"I'll give my son to ransom all mankind!"
O what a bargain! are men's souls like sheep
To buy and sell, the fattest for best price,
In open market, that and that for this
And one to make the weight up! . . .
       I'll not take
To cheat as he did like a petty fraud
In any German mart, who bawls a cure
For warts or corns or ringworm, which, applied,
Has not more skill than stupid faith can give it. . . .

For now I say, God did not give his son,
Christ did not sell his soul—he never paid it—
Though promises in trade are not less binding
To honest men—or Gods—than written paper,
And some would say, more sacred—not so he
That is most sacred—some say—Jesus the Christ!
Therefore shall Faustus that has sucked the world
As children suck an orange, cast away
The dried and bitter husk and embrace Hell. . . .

What doth it profit him—some writer saith—
To gain the world if he shall lose his soul?
Now Faustus, you can tell him! Tell him then
What you have lost and gained, and strike a balance;
Faustus hath lost a problematical soul—
(For who has seen it? I have never seen it!)
And gained the world and made the world his treasure; . . .

      I have tied to stars
The tails of stars and set the heaven fighting;
I've set new suns ashining in black night. . . .

No, stars are small talk, let's have what's important,
Let's talk of whores and harlots, ay by Christ
I'll talk round them till twilight or deep night
And so through bright till morning, nor be done! . . .

Then follow me, my whore, you maddening Helen,
You Helen draped in what my kisses gave you,
What my caresses clothed you with, a cloak
Cut of a lecherous cloth, soft as a cat's throat, made
Of kisses and caresses covering your limbs;
Now Christ envy me, she is my mate,
The Devil gave her to me body and soul,
And you can have her soul, my covetous Christ! . . .

                              Let me die!
I'll not have virgin's bastards saving me!
Conceived of the Holy Ghost! Here's something new
When ghosts can bed with virgins and get gods. . . .

                    Well, I have tweaked his nose,
His phantom nose—or have I rather tweaked
A member not as pointed, but as big?
I think I have, I think so! Spirit of God
That loves a maid as I do, what have I done
But tweaked your ghostly member for your pains?
I'll swear she squeaked, your virgin, though you are
Not more substantial than my shadow is
And nothing like as constant. . . .

I will not praise him for the dance he's led me!
I will not even greet him with the day:
"Good morrow God, how doth your garden prosper!" . . .

Great Lucifer shall be my overlord, . . .
Ha! with the legions there we'll conquer Heaven
And make another Hell, and God can have it!
What is this vaunted Heaven of my Christ
That I should not renounce it, renounce it all,
And spit on that same Christ who would not save me? . . .

Now Lucifer that art the scourge of God
Make me thy whip's end, and my soul the knot
That teases him; I'll not be lost in vain!
God's own enthronèd son cause shall admit
To cool my lips in Hell with his cool hand
But he shall dare not, knowing my teeth that bite
Will open wounds again he had forgot
Because the world had. . . .

I am resigned; let midnight come and go,
Let Christ that has condemned me, see me die;
I'll not cry out as he did, "God! my God!"
He'll see no coward, calling on the host of Heaven! . . .

                          Midnight is coming!
Lucifer is coming from deep Hell! Ah Christ,
I loved you once, or said so; were you deceived?
Then be so now and save me from deep Hell! . . .
                          O Christ save!
God's son save me, hold off this devil's whore,
Helen from Hell, 'tis he, 'tis Lucifer,
He bears her limbs and likeness, O my God!
Those limbs curl under me, he is at my heart,
He is cutting off my life's beat through her hands! . . .

Mother of God!
Tear off the hands, the hands of Lucifer,
He has worn the shape of Helen out of Hell
And now her breasts are brilliant with my blood
It falls upon them where my kisses fell,
Staining her flesh . . . what is it I am saying?
Where is the sun? Oh, it is midnight surely;
I thought it was the day—but I am dying;
O Jesus Christ forgive me, I am dying!
O mother forget your son!

              Johann Faustus is dead.

LP-43: LLEWELYN POWYS TO KENNETH HOPKINS

                                        [Clavadel
New Year morning before I have   January 2, 1939]
    spoken or written one word
        in this year
        1939
My dear Kenneth Hopkins,
    Thank you for your excellent letter and the poem the
beginning of which I liked very well indeed and I beg you
to continue in this same vein *to the very end* and scrap this
morbid Christian reaction and repentance. Remodel it en-

tirely—Let it be Promethean *up to the very end*—let **God** know that for once he has caught a dauntless weasel or wild cat by the scruff, the temper of whose spirit nothing will appease or affright but will spit and bite up to the last and knows it was worth it—remembering the sweetness of his *free* days upon the earth, his spiritual enfranchisement by forest and sea shore and within the rampart of topless cities. And above all how the gentleness and generosity of his darling and the wild play they had had together, her *cunning to be strange in bed* in their embraces make God the ghost and his son and all (their) his designs for man's redemption or man's torture not worth *a cab of Pigeon's dung*—I think you could write a long and noble and most notable poem on these lines. I regard this as a false start, like the false nest the wren is rumoured to build. I am in bed but in no bad way.

Good luck for the year.

Yours

Llewelyn Powys

I think you have a wonderful chance here to make a new powerful Faustus last scene in a truly modern form—Let it be a fine bold championship of the world of *the sense and the senses* against superstition and the values of the spirit—Make it proud—orgulous up to the last moment—blasphemous and saucy with references to the "covetous Christ" and his "tall cross" and "spitting" and "biting the hand of God for his pity" and let all your sympathy and tenderness be for the girl and all your aesthetic appreciations for grass and sea foam and toad-stools and sheep bells and hedge sticks and apples and attics and clouds and mackerel—and let him laugh at the frights of hell and give death pepper in the nose.

[On the flap side of the envelope, in Hopkins' hand]

Here's pepper for the nose of God—
Now let him sneeze a world off!

LP-44: LLEWELYN POWYS TO KENNETH HOPKINS

[Postcard:
Clavadel,
February 6, 1939]

Thank you for your letter. I have not been well. I was interested and pleased with the page of poetry you sent me—Surely I would be willing to subscribe 10/- towards its appearance. I thought the photograph you so kindly sent me very charming, especially so in its rural setting. I was very happy to hear of your success with Time and Tide.[1] Good luck!

Yours sincerely
Llewelyn Powys

LP-45: LLEWELYN POWYS TO KENNETH HOPKINS

[Design of ankh, in ink]

Clavadel
Davos Platz
Switzerland
April 6, 1939

Dear Kenneth Hopkins,
Thank you very much for sending me this poem—I think in a general way it is notable and does you credit—but re-

---

[1] Kenneth Hopkins' first sale—"two and a half guineas, less the agent's ten percent," for a short story, "The Parrot," in the April 22 issue of *Time and Tide*. In the letters from Wales congratulating him on the sale—and on a new job, traveling for a publishing firm—John Cowper Powys made some comparisons:

[We] were discussing your essential character *as a poet* and we decided that, like Uncle John, you possess a certain detachment and self-centeredness—and also a certain cunning—and also a certain *fight* in you that these sensitive artists lack—but that Christopher Marlowe and indeed, tho' he's rather *different,* Louis Marlow possessed and possess[es]—and Keats himself.

An earlier letter makes a physical comparison: "Do you know we've decided that you have an Elizabethan countenance that we can well imagine over a ruff! Your long narrow chin is *just* like a picture I've seen of Sir Philip Sidney.

garding it with a stricter eye and from a wider point of view I am not really content with it. [the expanded "Faustus"]

It seems to me to be youthful—It makes up in violence what it lacks in depth. I am sure your conventional ending is a mistake—an intransigent ending alone justifies the poem—the penitent's panic has been done before and done better.

My feeling is that you should think only of your Betty when you write of Helen—remember her "step on the stair" and use *her* as the supreme revelation whereby Faustus was led to understand the prides of Prometheus—Let him meet his fate with indifference and haughty resignation *because it had been worth it*——worth it, the hours he had spent on the corn-bearing earth that had been to him no metaphysical *shadow-land—worth it* when he had caught her and had her under the skeleton elders near the White Nose—worth it when he had listened to the rain on the window and her fast asleep breathing—as he lay by her, himself wide staring, awake, in a little attic with measureless stars above the roof. I think the poem is too traditional—too practical, *not personal enough*—I think your Betty should be far more its inspiration—I dislike its ending with its mean cringing *from the bottom of my heart*—besides you play upon an old note here "See where Christ's blood streams in the Universe!"[1] I think the poem should be much more broadly beamed—I think the *real* should be much more profoundly juxtaposed against the ideal—the natural against the theological—man against God!

If the poem is considered more particularly I think it contains promise and some twenty fine lines—and literary conceits—I do not like the word "compromise" to be used in this connection—I think some word like "shift" would be better. I liked the passage about the "German market" and the chapman. "Goods" has too modern a connotation for my liking—too American—"wares" would be better.— That "suck an orange" is too common an expression and an anachronism—I would substitute "the gospel" for "some writer" the quotation being so well known.—I don't like the "small talk." "Let's talk of punks and harlots" whats the

---

[1] "See, see where Christ's blood streams in the Firmament!"—from the final speech of Marlowe's Faustus.

difference between whores and harlots? I liked the furious insolence of the three lines beginning "I took a journey"— but many will not. *Summoned* is too heavy—I myself cannot abide the erotic association of blood and tears. I am myself a sunshine lover. I like the lines beginning "Then follow me my whore" as much as any in the poem—especially "soft as a cat's throat." I do not object to the blasphemy of the "tweaked member," and like the use—the daring use of such words as "squeaked." I like "Good morrow God how doth your garden prosper!" I like the echo of Marlowe in such lines "Ha! With the legions"—The three lines beginning "Now Lucifer" I like passing well but the last pages not at all—They do not seem to me deeply felt or deeply imaginative—the horror strikes me as artificial after the bragging and unnatural and the talk of blood and sweat, and tears unpleasantly and morbidly and vulgarly Christian. I like the use of the word "curled" for Helen and that is all.

I enclose half a guinea as I promised.

Yours sincerely
Llewelyn Powys

In "The Moods of Faustus"—in its composition and first mailing to Switzerland, in its revision, in the two long critiques—a primary contrast between Kenneth Hopkins and Llewelyn Powys becomes clearer—a contrast that has nothing to do with class, age, schooling, or religion. The contrast is in the cast of mind of the two men—their different views on the function of poetry. Powys, born before Arnold's death, saw a vital use for poetry; he preached his ideas as consistently as any writer of English literature who lived into the twentieth century. No one of the thirty-odd books that carry his name—indeed, almost no chapter in these books—is sermonless. To his prose he brought the skill of a Taylor and a Donne, and all the fervor of seventeenth-century nonconformists.

Hopkins still holds with Flecker's central maxim. "I go to poetry for beauty first," he wrote to A. E. Coppard during a debate-by-letter during 1937 and 1938. "And wisdom, or even sense, I accept if present, and do without if absent. As it happens, most good poetry does contain plenty of sense, and much wisdom too, but I am sure you can have poetry with neither." Flecker also pointed out, Hopkins reminded Coppard, that there was a genre and a platform for those who held otherwise—the sermon and the pulpit. Today he would little alter those statements. And of the ending of "The Moods of Faustus" he has said, while reading his lyrics at colleges in the Boston area in 1965, "despite Mr. Powys' impassioned words, I still think that this is how the character Faustus goes down."

LP-46: LLEWELYN POWYS TO KENNETH HOPKINS

[Clavadel]
June 14, 1939

My dear Kenneth Hopkins,

I must first thank you very much for your very well-selected gift that you were so kind as to send me. Miss Gregory was very happy with hers also—You are remarkably clever at finding just the book for the right person. The little Matthew Arnold you sent me some time ago has been very useful to me. I must also thank you for your last long and interesting letter with the enclosed sonnet—which I enjoyed reading—Yes, use the half guinea as seems best for forwarding your literary fortunes.

It is a great pleasure having Mr Wilkinson here—though the weather has not been too favourable and he was greatly displeased to wake one morning to find the valley white with snow. He is reading me chapters from his book[1] which I enjoy extremely—His own disposition is eighteenth century in its tastes and demeanour and this renders his task easy and excellent. I was interested to hear your news of Love and Death. The book has I think staying qualities but

---

[1] *Sackville of Drayton* (London, 1948).

I can hardly expect from its sales any remarkable rise in my fortunes.[2]

With my best wishes as always—

Yours
Llewelyn Powys

LP-47: LLEWELYN POWYS TO KENNETH HOPKINS

Clavadel
Davos Platz
Switzerland
August 14, 1939

Dear Mr Kenneth Hopkins,

It was good of you to remember my birthday—and I liked well the picture of the boats but not so much having to pay double for insufficient postage!

I hope very much all goes well with you. Mr Siberell sent me a paper containing one of your sonnets.

I crawl towards better health at a snail's pace—On the morning of the 13th I found a little snail crawling on my counterpane and took it as a good omen—its unexpected trespassing. I have been reading Candide again and Micromegas for the first time—This book in Everyman would please you. Miss Gregory has been reading me Marcel Proust and we have reached the last three volumes. He is to my mind by far the greatest writer of my generation—perhaps yours will do better. I was touched to see H. G. Wells' letter in Time and Tide—What buggers these young men are to torment so brave an old bully—The most foolish atheist is dearer to me than these fiddle faddling idealists

---

[2] Five days earlier he had written to his brother Littleton:
This hot weather . . . does not suit me too well . . . and I am disappointed a little about my book. It has had passionately enthusiastic reviews but after the first month has sold only 450 copies and this is a discouragement. I had rather hoped to be released for a time from the sweat of journalism! I know in my own mind it is far the best book I have written and I must console myself with this private knowledge and also with the appreciation *of the few.*

could ever be—I find them contemptible, Jung and all of
them. They always are popular—They always have the
crowd firm by the ear.
    Please give the enclosed to your Miss Betty.
                                    Yours sincerely
                                    Llewelyn Powys

    The contempt for Jung would seem to relate more to
his spiritual content than the analytic method. Writing
about himself for *Twentieth Century Authors* within a
month or two of this letter, Llewelyn listed Freud as one
of the five contemporaries who had most influenced him.
He had seen Freud in 1926 when, in Dorset, he and Alyse
Gregory received pleading and irrational telegrams (one
signed "Tolstoy," the other, "Clayfoot") from an American literary friend who was then Freud's patient; they
left immediately for Vienna—within the hour—but their
visit proved of little solace to the ill man. "[Freud]
treated us with great courtesy," Llewelyn wrote to his
eldest brother. "He was, I think, very much taken with
Alyse as though her firm dorian glances restored him in
a world of crooked complexes."
    The enclosure for Miss Betty was a small cameo—per-
haps one of Llewelyn's mother's—for in Hopkins' lost July
and August, 1939, letters to Davos Platz there certainly
were details about the impending marriage, now only two
weeks away. But from the evidence of the next letter,
there seems to have been no mention of international ten-
sion; even as Jane Austen's novels and almost all of her
correspondence neglect Napoleon, there is no talk of
Hitler and Chamberlain between Hopkins and Powys:

LP-48: LLEWELYN POWYS TO KENNETH HOPKINS

                                    [Clavadel
                                    August 28, 1939]
My dear Kenneth Hopkins,
    I thank you so much for the very attractive photograph—

It is the best I have ever seen of you—You surely look a light-heeled poet and with White Nose behind you—a seaside siskin, a sycamore seed turning in the wind! And I am greatly pleased to possess the delightful edition of Tusser. I have the valuable edition here with Rudyard Kipling's Introduction but it has never really been to my taste. You are a wonder at finding books. Mr Wilkinson speaks with astonishment of your genius with old book shops.

I liked your sonnet and especially that such thoughts and interests should be in your head, and not a mention of the crisis!—This struck me as the right and civilized attitude but revealing a high detachment that is beyond me—My own love of liberty and hatred of the herd and opposition to tyranny is so strong that against all sense I would resist these rascals but as the years come upon me I find myself growing foolish in more ways than one, crotchety-crabbed, often a very lunatic.

I am so glad you have had some good holidays. I do hope you will progress in the writing trade—I would be happy if you could win to your freedom here—I think you are right to try for it in all ways—I see no danger of your sinking back to what is second rate.

Please thank your Lady Betty for her message. We have some friends staying in the valley. I am I believe a little better, but have not yet reached a condition where I consider it is safe to walk much.

Yours,
Ll Powys

Within the week England declared war, and within three months, at Davos Platz on December 2, 1939, Llewelyn Powys was dead. Death came, ironically, not from the "little white worms" that he had fought for thirty years, but from a stomach hemorrhage. He was caught on the horns of a dietary dilemma: fighting consumption required rich, nourishing foods—foods that hastened the killing ulcer. At the very end, Miss Gregory wrote, "he said with a certain tender raillery, 'We shall all be dust soon.' "

9

Epilogue

Ten years after Llewelyn Powys' death, when the Bodley Head published an edition of *Advice to a Young Poet* containing forty-six letters from Powys to Kenneth Hopkins, *John O' London's Weekly* invited the recipient of the letters to review the book. The thirty-five-year-old poet responded in the issue of May 27, 1949:

Letters to a Poet

By Kenneth Hopkins

To read a group of letters in print, ten or a dozen years after receiving the originals, is a strange experience. Some time ago, when I saw the proofs, and more strongly now that I hold the published book, *Advice to a Young Poet*, by Llewelyn Powys (Bodley Head, 4s. 6d.), I wonder what manner of young man it was who received these pungent and uncompromising letters. And to-day, as I look back along the accidents of a decade, I can imagine the young man who was myself looking forward into an unpredictable future; but if he met my eyes he would think me a stranger.

As we develop and alter we seldom give a thought to the selves from which we are sprung, and that is why these letters in sober print recall me to what I supposed I had escaped from for ever—the young man at Bournemouth who wanted to be a writer.

It was from Bournemouth, that "fortress of unpoetical prosperity," as Powys called it, that I wrote asking if I could visit him; and it was to my home at Bournemouth that most of these letters were addressed. They were almost the only contact I had with the world of books and authors I was so anxious to enter. Llewelyn Powys was the first writer I ever met, and I could wish no young man better fortune than to meet such a man as he was.

I have vivid memories of the visits I made to the isolated cottages above East Chaldon where Llewelyn Powys lived with his wife, next door to his sister, and near his brothers John and Theodore. At that time he was almost always in bed when I visited him, for his health was giving considerable anxiety, and I can't recall that I ever saw him up and dressed. He looked usually as he does on the cover of this book, with his bright hair still curling, and the pointed beard and lined face framed in the old shawl that once belonged to Edward FitzGerald. Disease had not dimmed the searching gaze of his eyes, as I found out often enough when some piece of adolescent foolishness escaped me. I must have been an unpromising disciple, but his patience was unfailing, his encouragement never wtihheld.

It was almost by chance—a very fortunate chance for me— that I had written to him. I had read one, or perhaps two, of his books, and had admired them; but at that time I was much more under the influence of such writers as Belloc and Chesterton, whose appeal is so strong for boys in their teens. I would have been delighted to visit either of them.

But the impressive personality of Llewelyn Powys, and the sunny, uncomplicated philosophy he taught me, if they did not completely replace these writers in my affection, at least checked their influence, and looking back I am glad now that this was so. He helped me to appreciate the things I took for granted—had I not been born within sound of the sea? yet he taught me to look at it for the first time. He taught me to appreciate books I had condemned unread, to value qualities in men and life that I had considered commonplace or negligible. And the eloquence and the poetry of his writings won me for ever from the facile wit I had formerly thought the best that contemporary letters could offer.

Another new volume in the uniform edition of Llewelyn Powys's works is *Glory of Life* and *Now That the Gods Are Dead* (Bodley Head, 4s. 6d.) . These two essays contain the mature expression of his philosophy in his most eloquent prose, and even readers who deny everything he affirms will delight in the subtle and beautiful writing of this small book.

One day, fifteen years ago, Llewelyn Powys gave me a copy of *Impassioned Clay*, the longest and finest of his philosophical essays, inscribing it with a quotation taken from the body of the book: "By day and by night, no sight that we see, but has its own poetical burden." I had never read anything like this before, and I read on and on, when I returned home, amazed and uplifted. This book, more than anything I read in my teens, turned my thoughts from the commonplace, the merely ephemeral, to the permanently valuable in literature. It is intrinsically a fine essay; but this apart, it led me to such writers as Rabelais, Lucretius, Montaigne, of whom I had scarcely heard even the names. And how stirring to a young man was its own message!

"I appeal to youth, to boys and girls with senses uncorrupted, with senses fair and fresh. Do not be deceived, do not listen to the foolish talk of envious old women and of fearful, defeated old men. The days of your youth are yours, the hours of your youth are yours, so few so few." I determined that here was the preacher for me, and no influence in the impressionable years around twenty was stronger in me than his. His books, his conversation, his letters, opened to me a new and larger world. His conversation, lively, wise, penetrating, is ended for ever, but the writings that are so faithful a reflection of his spirit are available to any: "His back is turn'd, but not his brightness hid."

In these letters I find again and again, as I re-read them, them, advice and admonition which with fifteen years' advantage over the recipient I can now see to be good. "I thought so then, but now I know it."

This is advice not only for young poets, but for young men and young women of every sort who want to make the best of their lives. How much I was able to profit from it I am unable to tell, but by whatever degree I failed, I know I am now the poorer. Yet as I read them again in print, I find in these letters many things from which it is not too late for me to reap advantage.

Bibliography

BOOKS BY LLEWELYN POWYS
A check list in chronological order

Confessions of Two Brothers. By John Cowper Powys and Llewellyn [*sic*] Powys. Rochester, New York: The Manas Press, 1916.

Ebony and Ivory. Preface by Theodore Dreiser. New York: American Library Service, 1923.

———. Preface by Edward Shanks. London: Grant Richards, 1923.

———. Revised. Harmondsworth, Middlesex: Penguin Books Ltd., 1939.

———. Introduction by Louis U. Wilkinson. [A mutilated text incorporating some of the 1939 revisions.] London: Richards Press, 1960.

Thirteen Worthies. Preface by Van Wyck Brooks. New York: American Library Service, 1923.

———. Preface by Van Wyck Brooks. London: Grant Richards, 1924.

Black Laughter. New York: Harcourt, Brace and Co., 1924.

———. London: Grant Richards, 1925.

———. Reprinted in the Travellers' Library. London: Jonathan Cape, 1929.

———. Introduction by Negley Farson. London: Macdonald, 1953.

Honey and Gall. Girard, Kansas: Haldeman-Julius Company, 1924.

Cup-Bearers of Wine and Hellebore. Girard, Kansas: Haldeman-Julius Company, 1924.

Skin for Skin. New York: Harcourt, Brace and Co., 1925.

———. London: Jonathan Cape, 1927.

The Verdict of Bridlegoose. New York: Harcourt, Brace and Co., 1926.

———. London: Jonathan Cape, 1927.

Henry Hudson. London: John Lane The Bodley Head, 1927.

———. New York: Harper and Brothers, 1928.

Out of the Past. Pasadena, California: Grey Bow Press, n.d. [ca. 1928]

The Cradle of God. New York: Harcourt, Brace and Co., 1929.

———. London: Jonathan Cape, 1929.

———. Introduction by Ernest Carr. London: Watts and Co., 1949.

The Pathetic Fallacy. London: Longmans, Green and Company, 1930.

———. Reprinted in the Thinker's Library. London: Watts and Co., 1931.

An Hour on Christianity. [Published in England as *The Pathetic Fallacy.*] Philadelphia: J. B. Lippincott Company, 1930.

Apples Be Ripe. New York: Harcourt, Brace and Co., 1930.

———. London: Longmans, Green and Company, 1930.

———. Reprinted in Big Ben Books. London: Wells, Gardner, Darton, and Co., 1940.

A Pagan's Pilgrimage. New York: Harcourt, Brace and Co., 1931.

———. London: Longmans, Green and Company, 1931.

Impassioned Clay. Woodcut by Lynd Ward. New York: Longmans, Green and Company, 1931.

———. [The English edition lacks the woodcut.] London: Longmans, Green and Company, 1931.

The Life and Times of Anthony à Wood. An abridgment of Andrew Clark's edition, edited and with an introduction by Llewelyn Powys. London: Wishart and Co., 1932.

———. Reprinted in The World's Classics. London: Oxford University Press, 1961.

Now That the Gods Are Dead. Engravings by Lynd Ward. New York: Equinox Press, 1932.

Glory of Life. Engravings by Robert Gibbings. London: Golden Cockerel Press, 1934.

———. [Without the engravings] London: John Lane The Bodley Head, 1938.

Earth Memories. Woodcuts by Gertrude Mary Powys. London: John Lane The Bodley Head, 1934.

Damnable Opinions. London: Watts and Co., 1935.

Dorset Essays. Photographs by Wyndham Goodden. London: John Lane The Bodley Head, 1935.

The Twelve Months. Engravings by Robert Gibbings. London: John Lane The Bodley Head, 1936. [A limited, and a trade edition.]

Somerset Essays. Photographs by Wyndham Goodden. London: John Lane The Bodley Head, 1937.

Rats in the Sacristy. Preface by John Cowper Powys; engravings by Gertrude Mary Powys. London: Watts and Co., 1937.

The Book of Days. Compiled by John Wallis; etchings by Elizabeth Corsellis. London: Golden Cockerel Press, 1937.

Earth Memories. Introduction by Van Wyck Brooks. [This American edition also includes *Out of the Past* and selected essays from *Dorset Essays.*] New York: W. W. Norton and Co., 1938.

Love and Death. Introduction by Alyse Gregory. London: John Lane The Bodley Head, 1939.

————. Introduction by Alyse Gregory. New York: Simon and Schuster, 1941.

A Baker's Dozen. Introduction by Lloyd Emerson Siberell; illustrations by Mathias Noheimer. Herrin, Illinois: Trovillion Private Press, 1939.

————. Introduction by John Cowper Powys; decorations by Gertrude Mary Powys. London: John Lane The Bodley Head, 1941.

Old English Yuletide. Introduction by Violet and Hal W. Trovillion. [These two essays appeared in *A Baker's Dozen.*] Herrin, Illinois: Trovillion Private Press, 1940.

The Letters of Llewelyn Powys. Edited by Louis Wilkinson; introduction by Alyse Gregory. London: John Lane The Bodley Head, 1943.

Swiss Essays. London: John Lane The Bodley Head, 1947.

Advice to a Young Poet. London: John Lane The Bodley Head, 1949.

Llewelyn Powys: A Selection from his Writings. Edited by

Kenneth Hopkins. [Contains previously unpublished letters and essays as well as the selections from earlier works.] London: Macdonald, 1952.

————. New York: Horizon Press, 1961.

Note: The Bodley Head issued six of Powys' works—in four volumes—in a Uniform Edition:

Skin for Skin and The Verdict of Bridlegoose. London, 1948.

Glory of Life and Now That the Gods Are Dead. London, 1949.

Advice to a Young Poet. London, 1949.

Love and Death. London, 1950.

Macdonald issued one double volume:

Somerset and Dorset Essays. Foreword by John Cowper Powys. London, 1957.

BOOKS BY KENNETH HOPKINS

This chronological check list extends Anthony Newnham's A Check-List of Kenneth Hopkins published by The Humanities Research Center of the University of Texas in 1961.

Noms de plume appear in quotation marks at the end of an entry; the books by Hopkins signed "Warwick Mannon" and "Arnold Meredith" were part of a series in which the other authors used the same names.

The first five publications were privately printed; Grasshopper Press was Hopkins'.

Twelve Poems. Bournemouth, 1937.

Recent Poetry. Bournemouth, 1937.

New Sonnets. Bournemouth, 1938.

Six Sonnets. Bournemouth, 1938.

A Night Piece. Derby, 1943.

The Younger Sister. Derby: Grasshopper Press, 1944.

Love and Elizabeth. London: Sylvan Press, 1944.

Miscellany Poems. London: Grasshopper Press, 1946.

Songs and Sonnets. London: Grasshopper Press, 1947.

Vice Versa. London: World Film Publications, 1947. "Warwick Mannon."

Poems on Several Occasions. London: Grasshopper Press, 1948.

Spring in Park Lane. London: World Film Publications, 1948. "Warwick Mannon."

Miranda. London: World Film Publications, 1948. "Warwick Mannon."

No Room at the Inn. London: World Film Publications, 1948. "Warwick Mannon."

The Guinea Pig. London: World Film Publications, 1948. "Arnold Meredith."

Bond Street. London: World Film Publications, 1948. "Warwick Mannon."

To a Green Lizard Called Ramorino. London: Faun Press, 1949.

Bridal Song for Helen. London: Faun Press, 1949.

To a Green Lizard. London: Grasshopper Press, 1949.

Apes and Elderberries. London: Grasshopper Press, 1950. Published anonymously.

Walter de la Mare. London: Longsmans, Green and Company for The British Council, 1953.

The Corruption of a Poet. London: James Barrie, 1954.

The Poets Laureate. London: The Bodley Head, 1954.

———. New York: Library Publishers, 1955.

———. With a new preface. Carbondale: Southern Illinois University Press, 1966.

The Girl Who Died. London: Macdonald, 1955.

Helen of Troy. London: Beverley Books, 1956. "Christopher Adams."

Safari. London: Beverley Books, 1956. "Paul Marsh."

Inca Adventure. London: Chatto and Windus, 1956.

Great Moments in Exploration. London: Phoenix House, 1956.

———. New York: Roy Publishers, 1956.

The Liberace Story. London: Beverley Books, 1957. "Anton Burney." [Not distributed]

English Literature for Fun. London: Hutchinson, 1957. "Christopher Adams."

She Died Because . . . . London: Macdonald, 1957.

———. New York: Holt, Rinehart and Winston, 1964.

Portraits in Satire. London: Barrie Books, 1958.

———. New York: Barnes & Noble, Inc., 1959.
The Forty-First Passenger. London: Macdonald, 1958.
Dead against My Principles. London: Macdonald, 1960.
———. New York: Holt, Rinehart and Winston, 1963.
Tales of Ambledown Airport No. 1. Colin's Lucky Day. London: Hutchinson, 1960. "Edmund Marshall."
Tales of Ambledown Airport No. 2. The Missing Viscount. London: Hutchinson, 1960. "Edmund Marshall."
Pierce with a Pin. London: Macdonald, 1960.
Poor Heretic. Austin, Texas: University of Texas Press, 1961.
———. London: Putnam, 1962.
Foundlings & Fugitives. Austin, Texas: The Brick Row Book Shop, 1961.
42 Poems. London: Putnam, 1961.
Body Blow. London: Macdonald, 1962.
———. New York: Holt, Rinehart and Winston, 1965.
A Trip to Texas. London: Macdonald, 1962.
English Poetry: A Short History. Philadelphia: J. B. Lippincott Company, 1963.
———. London: Phoenix House, 1963.
———. London: Readers' Union, 1964.
Campus Corpse. London: Macdonald, 1963.
Collected Poems: 1935–1965. Carbondale: Southern Illinois University Press, 1964.
Amateur Agent. London: Boardman, 1964. "Christopher Adams."
The Powys Brothers: A Biographical Appreciation. London: Phoenix House, 1967.
The Powys Brothers: A Biographical Appreciation. Cranbury: Fairleigh Dickinson Press, 1968.
Poems: English and American. Houston, Texas: Brick Row Book Shop, 1968.

Books Edited or with Introductions
by Kenneth Hopkins

The English Lyric: A Selection. Brussels: de Visscher, 1945.
Edmund Blunden: A Selection of his Poetry and Prose. London: Hart-Davis, 1950.
———. New York: Horizon Press, 1962.

Llewelyn Powys: A Selection from his Writings. London: Macdonald, 1952.

———. New York: Horizon Press, 1961.

H. M. Tomlinson: A Selection from his Writings. London: Hutchinson, 1953.

Walter de la Mare: A Selection from his Writings. London: Faber and Faber, 1953.

The Worst English Poets. London: Wingate, 1958. "Christopher Adams."

A Little Treasury of Familiar Verse. London: John Baker, 1963.

A Little Treasury of Love Lyrics. London: John Baker, 1963.

A Little Treasury of Religious Verse. London: John Baker, 1964.

A Little Treasury of Familiar Prose. London: John Baker, 1964.

John Cowper Powys: A Selection from his Poems. London: Macdonald, 1964.

———. Hamilton, New York: Colgate University Press, 1965.

The Search: Fourth Series. Edited by Georgia Winn; Preface by Kenneth Hopkins. Carbondale: Southern Illinois University, 1964.

Crusade Against Crime. Edited by Jerry D. Lewis; introduction by Kenneth Hopkins. London: Boardman, 1965.

Crusade Again Crime, II. Edited by Jerry D. Lewis; introduction by Kenneth Hopkins. London: Boardman, 1965.

The Poetry of Railways. London: Frewin, 1966.

Issued by the Folio Society, London,
with Introductions by Kenneth Hopkins

Maupassant, Guy de. *Bel-Ami.* 1954.

Eden, Emily. *The Semi-Attached Couple.* 1955.

Surtees, R. S. *Hawbuck Grange.* 1955.

De La Mare, Walter. *Ghost Stories.* 1956.

Surtees, R. S. *Hillingdon Hill.* 1956.

Fielding, Henry. *Tom Jones.* 1959.

Defoe, Daniel. *Journal of the Plague Year.* 1960.

Henry, O. *Selected Stories.* 1960.

Peacock, Thomas. *Crotchet Castle.* 1964.

GENERAL BIBLIOGRAPHY

Alyse Gregory

The Day is Gone. New York: E. P. Dutton & Company, Inc., 1948.
"A Famous Family," *London Magazine,* V (March, 1958), 44–53.
Hester Craddock. London: Longmans, Green and Company, 1931.
King Log and Lady Lea. London: Constable and Company, 1929.
She Shall Have Music. New York: Harcourt, Brace and Company, 1926.
Wheels on Gravel. London: John Lane The Bodley Head, 1938.

John Cowper Powys

Autobiography. A new edition with introductions by J. B. Priestley and R. L. Blackmore. London: Macdonald; Hamilton, New York: Colgate University Press, 1967.
Enjoyment of Literature. New York: Simon and Schuster, 1938.
Letters of John Cowper Powys to Louis Wilkinson: 1935–1956. Edited by Louis Wilkinson. London: Macdonald, 1958; Hamilton, New York: Colgate University Press, 1966.
Maiden Castle. A new edition with an introduction by Malcolm Elwin. London: Macdonald; Hamilton, New York; Colgate University Press, 1966.

Littleton Powys

The Joy of It. London: Chapman & Hall Ltd., 1937.
Still the Joy of It. London: Macdonald, 1956.

Louis Umfreville Wilkinson
"Louis Marlow"

The Brothers Powys. Winston-Salem: The Press of John Wesley Clay, 1946. [A paper read to the Royal Society

of Literature by Louis Wilkinson. All other Wilkinson
entries are signed with the *nom de plume*, Louis Marlow.]
Forth, Beast! London: Faber and Faber, 1946.
Seven Friends. London: Richards Press, 1953.
Swan's Milk. London: Faber and Faber, 1934.
Welsh Ambassadors: Powys Lives and Letters. London: Chapman & Hall Ltd., 1936.

Others

Agate, James. *Ego 5.* London: George G. Harrap & Co. Ltd.,
1943.
————. *Ego 6.* London: George G. Harrap & Co. Ltd., 1944.
Baedeker, Karl. *Switzerland.* Twenty-third edition. Leipzig:
Karl Baedeker, Publisher, 1909.
Cecil, David. *The Stricken Deer.* Indianapolis: The Bobbs-
Merrill Company, 1930.
Churchill, R. C. "Not Least Llewelyn," *A Review of English
Literature,* IV (January, 1963), 68–75.
————. *The Powys Brothers.* London: Longmans, Green and
Company for The British Council, 1962.
Elwin, Malcolm. "John Cowper Powys," *Writers of To-Day.*
Edited by Denys Val Baker. London: Sidgwick & Jackson,
1948, 117–134.
————. *The Life of Llewelyn Powys.* London: John Lane
The Bodley Head, 1946.
————. "Llewelyn Powys," *Voices* (Autumn, 1946). Edited
by Denys Val Baker. 71–77.
Everybody's Weekly. London: January, 1949, to December,
1951.
Gardiner, Alan Henderson. "Egypt: Ancient Religion." *Encyclopaedia Britannica* (11th ed.), IX, 48–57.
Grainger, Boyne. *The Hussy.* New York: Boni and Liveright,
1924.
————. *The Jester's Reign.* New York: Carrick & Evans, 1938.
Hamilton, Edith. *The Greek Way.* New York: W. W. Norton
& Company, 1930.
Hauri, J., and others. *Davos as Health Resort.* Davos: Davos
Printing Company, Ltd., 1906.

Joost, Nicholas. *Scofield Thayer and The Dial*. Carbondale, Illinois: Southern Illinois University Press, 1964.

Knight, G. Wilson. *The Saturnian Quest*. London: *Methuen & Co. Ltd.*, 1964.

Kunitz, Stanley J., and Howard Haycraft (eds.). *Twentieth Century Authors*. New York: The H. W. Wilson Co., 1942.

Lucretius. *On the Nature of Things*. Translated by Cyril Bailey. Oxford: The Clarendon Press, 1910.

Mann, Thomas. "The Making of 'The Magic Mountain,'" *Atlantic Monthly*, Vol. 191 (January, 1953), 41–45.

Millay, Edna St. Vincent. *Letters of Edna St. Vincent Millay*. Edited by Allan Ross Macdougall. New York: Harper & Brothers, 1952.

Miller, Henry. "The Immortal Bard," *A Review of English Literature*, IV (January, 1963), 21–24.

Montaigne, Michel de. *Selected Essays*. The Charles Cotton–W. Hazlitt Translation, edited by Blanchard Bates. New York: The Modern Library, 1949.

Newnham, Anthony. *A Check-List of Kenneth Hopkins*. Austin, Texas: The Humanities Research Center of the University of Texas, 1961.

Norman, Charles. "E. E. Cummings, Notes toward a Final Chapter," *The Texas Quarterly*, VII (Winter, 1964), 87–94.

Page, William (ed.). *The Victoria History of Somerset, II*. London: Constable and Company, 1911.

Priestley, J. B. "The Happy Introvert," *A Review of English Literature*, IV (January, 1963), 25–32.

Quinlan, Maurice J. *William Cowper*. Minneapolis: The University of Minnesota Press, 1953.

Sherman, Stuart P. *Critical Woodcuts*. New York: Charles Scribner's Sons, 1926.

Sims, G. F. *A Catalogue of the Llewelyn Powys Manuscripts*. Hurst, Berkshire: G. F. Sims, 1953.

Singleton, Esther (ed.). *Switzerland as Described by Great Writers*. New York: Dodd, Mead and Company, 1908.

Southey, Robert. *The Lives and Works of the Uneducated*

ography* 207

Poets. Edited by J. S. Childers. London: Humphrey Milford, 1925.

Symonds, John Addington, and his daughter Margaret. *Our Life in the Swiss Highlands*. Second edition. London: Adam and Charles Black, 1907.

Taylor, Warner (ed.). *Types and Times in the Essay*. New York: Harper & Brothers, 1932.

Ward, Richard Heron. *The Powys Brothers*. London: John Lane The Bodley Head, 1935.

Wasserstrom, William. *The Time of The Dial*. Syracuse University Press, 1963.

Weigand, Hermann J. *Thomas Mann's Novel Der Zauberberg*. New York: D. Appleton–Century Company, 1933.

Wilson, Angus. " 'Mythology' in John Cowper Powys's Novels," *A Review of English Literature*, IV (January, 1963), 9–20.

Index

Ackland, Valentine, 67–68, 110
Akhenaton, 23, 66, 99
Alexandra, Queen, 65
Allingham, William, 55
Ankh (Llewelyn Powys' colophon), 24, 57, 187
Anstey, Christopher, 40
Archer, E. (Mrs. Charles Lahr), 173
Aristippus, 66
Arnold, Matthew, 86, 89, 91, 153, 161, 165, 189, 190
Atlantic Monthly, 63
Aurora Leigh (E. B. Browning), 38
Austen, Jane, 192
Austen, John, 128
Austin, Alfred, 40
Autobiography of Benvenuto Cellini, 54

Baring, Maurice, 120, 147
Barnett, Vincent, 17
Bate, Walter Jackson, 17, 137
Bayly, Thomas Haynes, 39
Beardsley Period, The, (Burdett), 105
Beith, Janet, 119
Belloc, Hilaire, 40, 76, 96, 195
Benét, Stephen Vincent, 148
Besant, Sir Walter, 148
Biographia Britannica, 169
Blackmore, Sir Richard, 39
Blackmore, Richard Doddridge, 59–60

Blackthorn Winter, The (Philippa Powys), 43, 129
Blake, William, 76, 113
Blunden, Edmund, 40
Boswell, James, 141
Brautigam, Herman, 17
Brick Row Book Shop (Houston), 37
Bridges, Robert, 39
Brontës, the, 41
Brooke, Rupert, 96, 130
Brooks, Van Wyck, 102, 116, 117, 152
Brown, Bruce, 17
Browning, Elizabeth Barrett, 38
Browning, Robert, 37–39
Bunyan, John, 122
Burney, Anton (pseudonym used by Kenneth Hopkins), 37
Burns, Robert, 148
Burton, Robert, 62
Byron, George Gordon, sixth Baron, 76, 111

Calverley, Charles Stuart, 38
Cambridge University, 21, 56, 58, 61, 175
Candide (Voltaire), 191
Canterbury Tales, The, 121
Castorp, Hans, 16
Cellini, Benvenuto, 54
Cerne Giant, 113
Cervantes, Miguel de, 96, 109, 117, 161

209